THE
EVERYTHING®
— Series —

Dear Reader,

Growing up, we never thought we'd need to write our own marriage vows. We each assumed we would either marry someone from our own belief system (Episcopalian and *Star Trek*), or whoever we fell in love with would be so crazy about us that they'd forget their own silly ideas and get with the program.

Needless to say, Plan A fell through pretty quickly. We are two independent minds who needed to bend a bit. We finally did reach a compromise with the help of our clergyperson and our own bouts of soul-searching, but it wasn't always easy to embrace new ideas and let the old dreams die.

We hope that you will find in this book the ideas and inspiration you need to write the kinds of vows that represent your own unique relationship and love for each other, and that will help sustain you through the occasional rough patches ahead.

Happy Writing!

Don and Elizabeth

The EVERYTHING Series

These handy, accessible books give you all you need to tackle a difficult project, gain a new hobby, or even brush up on something you learned back in school but have since forgotten. You can read from cover to cover or just pick out information from our four useful boxes.

(E) Alerts: Urgent warnings

(E) Essentials: Quick handy tips

(E) Facts: Important snippets of information

(E) Questions: Answers to common questions

When you're done reading, you can finally say you know **EVERYTHING**®!

PUBLISHER Karen Cooper

DIRECTOR OF ACQUISITIONS AND INNOVATION Paula Munier

MANAGING EDITOR, EVERYTHING SERIES Lisa Laing

COPY CHIEF Casey Ebert

ACQUISITIONS EDITOR Katie McDonough

ASSOCIATE DEVELOPMENT EDITOR Elizabeth Kassab

EDITORIAL ASSISTANT Hillary Thompson

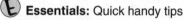

Visit the entire Everything® series at *www.everything.com*

THE
EVERYTHING®

WEDDING VOWS BOOK
3RD EDITION

How to personalize the most important promise you'll ever make

Don Lipper and Elizabeth Sagehorn

Avon, Massachusetts

An Everything® Series Book.
Everything® and everything.com® are registered
trademarks of F+W Media, Inc.

Published by Adams Media, an F+W Media Company
57 Littlefield Street, Avon, MA 02322 U.S.A.
www.adamsmedia.com

ISBN 10: 1-59869-861-3
ISBN 13: 978-1-59869-861-9

Printed in Canada.

J I H G F E D C B A

Library of Congress Cataloging-in-Publication Data
is available from the publisher.

This publication is designed to provide accurate and authoritative information with regard to the subject matter covered. It is sold with the understanding that the publisher is not engaged in rendering legal, accounting, or other
professional advice. If legal advice or other expert assistance is required, the
services of a competent professional person should be sought.
　　—From a *Declaration of Principles* jointly adopted by a Committee of the
American Bar Association and a Committee of Publishers and Associations

Many of the designations used by manufacturers and sellers to distinguish
their products are claimed as trademarks. Where those designations appear
in this book and Adams Media was aware of a trademark claim, the designations have been printed with initial capital letters.

This book is available at quantity discounts for bulk purchases.
For information, please call 1-800-289-0963.

Contents

Top Ten Sources of Inspiration for Writing Your Own Wedding Vows

1. The right music can be the perfect tool to get your head into the right writing place. While screenwriter Richard Curtis was working on *Love Actually*, he listened to Mariah Carey singing "All I Want for Christmas Is You" so often that he finally included it in the movie.

2. A witty romantic book with the requisite happy ending like *Pride and Prejudice* or *Jane Eyre* can get the vow-writing juices flowing.

3. Plan a unique day with your fiancé. Spending the day together will help you focus on why you're getting married.

4. Ask your parents and prospective in-laws about their courtships and marriages.

5. Do some volunteer work. Yeah, you're busy right now, but nothing gives you a fresh perspective like helping someone else.

6. Go someplace new. Go to that trade show in a part of the country you've never visited before and take an extra day to go sightseeing, or take a three-day (solo) cruise to go whale watching down Baja California.

7. Take a young person to an amusement park or an old person out to lunch. You'll walk away seeing the world through entirely different eyes.

8. Reread old diary entries to see how your ideas about romance and what constitutes the perfect mate have evolved.

9. Meditate. Scientists have discovered that when people stop actively thinking about something, they are more prone to having the "Eureka!" moment they have been searching for.

10. Every family has a self-appointed historian. Ask yours about some of the more interesting tales of romance and couplehood in your family tree.

Introduction

First of all, why not write your own vows?

Pessimists say that we often want to find a custom fit in an off-the-rack world. But when it comes to your wedding, shouldn't your vows be as unique as your love? Let's face it, every part of the modern wedding is a personal decision, and one size does not fit all. Every wedding is different, so why shouldn't the vows be as well?

There are many reasons why the traditional service might not fit your needs, but you don't need an excuse. Creating your own wedding vows has become part of the mainstream. In some circles it is almost expected. In the last fifty years, more and more couples have opted for "unique" weddings that include wholly created or modified traditional vows. Whichever approach you prefer, this book has got you covered.

If you just want to tweak the traditional vows, they're right here. If you want to look at traditional vows from other cultures for inspiration, they're here too. If the prospect of writing your vows makes you sweat, don't worry.

We've got you covered. Writing your own wedding vows is easy—if you know how.

There are a lot of myths about how hard it is to write. Sportswriter Red Smith famously said, "Writing is easy. I just sit down at the typewriter, cut open a vein, and bleed." Such imagery can strike terror in the calmest of minds. With a wedding date breathing down your neck, writing vows looks like a bullet you'd be smart to dodge. But there's a secret you don't know.

Writing your vows will be fun. Wedding planning requires a great deal of time, energy, and stress. Can you really add writing your own vows to this ever-expanding list of to-dos without exploding? Yes, you can. Writing your vows is kitten-play and this book will show you how to enjoy the process.

Writing your vows isn't a homework assignment. Think of it as a mental vacation from the everyday. Most people don't get a chance to have a creative outlet. They write e-mails, memos, and lists (lots of lists), but the last time they wrote anything vaguely creative was back in high school. Here's your chance to journey to new imaginative landscapes that you've long forgotten. Adding to the beauty of all this, your vows will be short—a minute or two tops. (Any longer and it will sound like an infomercial: "Let me tell you all the features you get with our love. Now how much would you pay?")

And here's the best part. Forget about every D you ever got for your deathless prose in school. This writing won't count toward your final grade as a spouse. Your vows are a statement of your love for each other and the life you plan to create together. There are no absolutes. We're grading on a curve and you are the ultimate authority of your vows. You are the one who will judge when it hits the mark. And if you follow the steps outlined here, you'll score a quick bull's-eye.

So you've got a prospect for a pleasurable activity that will bring the two of you closer together with absolutely no risk and the potential for a great reward. Once again, why not write your vows?

Let's start having some fun!

Chapter 1
Why Write Your Own Vows?

Planning a wedding can be a lot of hard work, but writing your vows shouldn't be. Here's where you and your intended will publicly declare your love for each other. The time you spend in crafting the words you speak is all about you. Forget about the seating arrangements, the bridesmaids' dresses, the caterer, the photographer, and all the money you've spent. As with many of the best things in life, wedding vows are absolutely free.

The Basics

Choosing to write your own vows shows that you are an independent and adventurous couple. This isn't about falling back on clichés or trying to do it the way it's done in the movies. Expressing your unique feelings is much more interesting and a hundred times more touching than any work of fiction.

ⓔ *Question?*

Can we write our own vows for any kind of wedding ceremony?
Before you get too far along in the process of creating a personalized vow, check with your ceremony officiant for guidelines on how to proceed. Different traditions take their own approach to the question of what should or should not be said at the altar. Be sure to resolve these important issues early in the process.

Perhaps the best way to get you started on the right foot is to revisit the dictionary definition of the word *vow*. According to Merriam-Webster, a vow is "a solemn promise or assertion . . . by which a person is bound to an act, service, or condition."

On the basis of this definition alone, the decision to write your own vows or adapt traditional vows makes perfect sense. After all, if you're binding yourself for life, shouldn't you have a say in what it is that you're binding yourself to? Not so long ago, wives were bound to obey their husbands. For hundreds of years no one gave that "obey" clause a second thought. It's only in recent times that people have begun to blaze their own trails.

When it comes to exchanging vows today, almost anything goes. Mixing and matching traditional vows, incorporating lines of poetry, or writing completely original material are all acceptable. The solemn nature of the vows, however, has not changed. You're still making a pledge before all and sundry, so keep this question in mind as you write: What exactly are you promising your betrothed?

Ⓔ *Essential*

If you're feeling a bit nervous, don't worry. Everyone who has ever attempted the daunting task of writing his own vows has experienced the same apprehension. Although your guests will be there to hear you speak your vows, this part of the ceremony is strictly between you and your intended. Listen to your heart, and the words will follow.

Personalizing Your Vows

Your wedding vows say a lot about who you and your fiancé are—and they'll most likely be short. You can use your vows to focus on certain aspects of your relationship or the wedding itself. You can also construct your vows in many different ways.

Place and Time Springboards

If there is anything significant about the place or time you are getting married, you might want to allude to it in your vows. In Chapter 6, you will find several sets of verses that can be adapted to specialized weddings, as well as dozens of other verses that may be appropriate for your situation. You can use or customize any of these verses, or you may decide the best way to emphasize the importance of the location is for you and your partner to compose an original poem of your own.

To generate ideas to write your vows, start thinking about the answers to the following questions. Why did you choose your location for your wedding? Did you choose a destination wedding because both of you love to travel? Did you choose a place close to home because it evokes all the memories of your relationship thus far? Why did you decide on your wedding date? Did it have anything to do with the season—the renaissance of spring, the glory of summer, the clarity of autumn, or the cold beauty of winter? Is it the month of your anniversary as a couple? Imagine the possibilities if both of your still-happily-married parents' weddings took place in the same month. Talk about carrying on an auspicious tradition!

Have Fun with Your Vows

Although this is no time to hone your stand-up routine, the natural course of the vow-composing process may lead you to certain statements that will bring a smile to your guests' lips. Perhaps the way you two met was funny, or maybe there's something amusing about your courtship or the location of your ceremony. Exchanging vows is a serious business, to be sure, but weddings are a celebration of life, so don't feel as if you have to mirror the often somber quality of traditional vows when you create your own.

Fact

Feel free to include some funny anecdote about how you two met, or how he proposed. Former president Bill Clinton allegedly proposed to his wife, Hillary, by saying that he had bought the house she liked and that she might as well marry him because he couldn't live in it alone.

One Shared Vow or Two Separate Vows?

When you write your own vows, you can each write your own or you can write one vow that both of you will say. Make the decision based on your personal preferences. Separate vows tend to be more personal, but a shared vow emphasizes your unity and commitment.

Two Vows with One Pen

Agreeing to make the same declaration is something akin to a joint mission statement, telling the world that you're of one mind on the subject of marriage. To be sure, this does not mean that one of you will do all the work and the other will take half the credit, but you might find that coming up with a single statement is considerably less time-consuming. It can make the vows sound equal, especially if one person in the marriage is not as strong a writer as the other.

Ⓔ *Essential*

If you want your vows to sound cohesive but don't want to say the exact same thing, you can agree on the basic structure but change the key words. Try something like the following: "What I love most about you is _____, _____, and _____. My hope for our future together is _____. I promise _____."

A Most Pleasant Surprise

On the other hand, if you want your declaration to seem unscripted and carry the stamp of spontaneity, you may decide to surprise your loved one on your wedding day. You need not go out of your way to carry out this sneak attack; simply insist upon writing your vows alone and agree not to disclose them until the grand unveiling. Of course, the surprise should go both ways, so you'll have to convince your fiancé to follow suit.

🄴 *Alert!*

Be sure that both of you agree to take the same tone in your vows. Remember the episode of *Friends* where Monica's girlfriends sighed wistfully over her romantic and touching words, while Chandler's guy friends gleefully chuckled over his amusing ones? You don't want to walk away from the altar disappointed in your fiancé's approach to vows.

Do It Together

Writing your wedding vows together can be an enlightening adventure. Plan to do something special together to create the mood, and get each other excited about it.

Set the scene for a romantic afternoon or evening. A clean, tidy space, some low-key mood music, and a supply of provisions are imperative. Incense and a candle or two wouldn't hurt either. Consider ordering a nice meal— creativity does not live on love alone.

🄴 *Essential*

Premarital counseling is a fantastic tool to shine a light on one's strengths and weaknesses. If you choose to have this discussion without a referee, topics like how you feel about love, marriage, commitment, and family should headline the conversation. It's this kind of insight that's going to make your vows stand out as a sincere pledge of allegiance.

A picnic is also a fun way to get your creative juices flowing. You can either surprise your partner or organize the outing together. Just remember, once you've laid out your spread and enjoyed the contents of your wicker basket, it's time to set to the task of composing your vows.

Decide whether you'll have one shared vow or two separate vows. If you will have two separate vows, will you allow your partner to read your vows before your wedding day? Look over the ideas in this book and decide what kind of vow you want. Do you like poetry, or would you rather start from scratch? Once you've settled all the major questions, you can start having some real fun. Regardless of whether you will share your vows with each other, brainstorm together and bounce ideas off of each other.

🔔 *The Right Words*

As you begin to write your vows, it's not unusual to find yourself at a loss for words. The following vocabulary list should help jump-start your thought process.

A	B	cherish
absolute	beauty	commitment
accomplish	bliss	companionship
adore	bond	confidant
affection		constant
ardor	C	content
attraction	caring	
	ceaseless	

D
dedication
destiny
divine

E
elation
embark
emotion
encourage
endless
enduring
eternity
everlasting
exquisite

F
faith
fidelity
fondly
forever
friend

G
genuine
gift
godly
grant
gravity

H
happiness
harmony
heart
honest
honor
humor

I
immortal
infinite
inspire
invaluable

J
join
joy
journey
jubilation

K
karma
key
kiss
knowledge

L
lasting
laughter
life
light

limitless
love
loyal

M
magical
meld
merge

N
never-ending
noble

O
oceanic
oneness
open
overcome

P
passion
perfection
pleasure
pledge
precious
promise
protect
provide
pure

Q
quality

R
radiant
real
rekindle
respect
responsibility

S
sacred
sacrifice
sanctity
selfless
share
soul
soul mate
strength
sublime
suited
support
sympathy

T
tender
thankful
total

treasure
true
trust

U
ultimate
understanding
unity
unparalleled
uplifting

V
value
vibrant
virtuous
vision
vivacious
vow

W
warm
whole
wisdom
worthy

Z
zeal
zenith

Chapter 2
Pen to Paper

Without further ado, it's time to roll up your sleeves, pick up a pen, and get down to the business of composing your masterpiece. Some people find it helpful to get into a creative mode by using a pen that is an unusual style or color. Heck, if crayons and butcher paper get you in the right space, raid the nearest preschool and let the fun begin.

Rule One: There Are No Rules

Using the material you have developed, start writing a first draft of your unique wedding vow.

Fact

You don't have to follow any rules, but it helps to be on the same wavelength as your fiancé. Your wedding vows are about the two of you and what you mean to each other, so they should complement each other.

Let yourself go—there is no right or wrong way to write your wedding vow. Give yourself permission to write anything and everything that seems right; you can always cut back later. Go ahead and wax rhapsodic. It's okay if this first draft runs long. Remember, it will take several drafts to develop a vow that is right for you.

After you've finished writing your first draft, read it over. While you may be able to reject some parts outright, at least a few phrases should smack of genuine feeling and stand out as vow-worthy. Highlight these gems for possible future use.

Seven Outlines to Get You Started

The first draft is all about jogging your imagination and sharpening your creative instincts. But let's face it; you're probably not going to want to recite it before a hundred of your nearest and dearest. What you need now is structure, and there's nothing like an outline to get your thoughts organized.

ⒺAlert!

The right way to compose your own wedding vows is your way. In customizing your own wedding vows, you should let your imagination be your guide. Develop vows that are meaningful to both you and your partner, that say something unique about your love, and that exemplify the way you envision your new life together.

Look at these outlines and examples simply as blueprints geared to get your vows up and running.

Outline One

Initial statement relating to the past.
Statement relating to your partner.
Promise or commitment to each other.

Here's an example:

- **Groom**: When I was a child, I thought nothing would ever persuade me to leave my home state of Maine when it came time to make my way in the world. But that was before I met you.
- **Bride**: As a young girl, I dreamed of a place where I could grow with another, step by step, side by side. I have found that place in your heart.
- **Groom**: Kathy, you have helped me to learn that love is a direction, not a destination.

- **Bride**: John, you have taught me that, when someone is there no matter what, trust and commitment come without effort of their own accord.
- **Groom**: I pledge to you my future. I will share all my tomorrows with you and no other.
- **Bride**: I pledge to you my future. I will share all my tomorrows with you and no other.

Outline Two
Extended statement culminating in a statement of your commitment to one another.

Here's an example:

- **Groom**: The first thing I noticed about Kathy was her radiant smile. We were both auditioning for a show in college, and when I asked her what type of piece she'd prepared, she said she planned to make it all up on the spot—and then she smiled at me. Kathy, your warmth and spontaneity have won my heart utterly. From this day forward, I will stand by your side. You are the one I will be true to always. Let us make our lives together.
- **Bride**: The first thing I noticed about John was his unceasing energy. As he waited for the director to call him in, he couldn't seem to sit still, and when I told him my plans for the audition, he stared at me as though I were mad—but mad in an interesting way. What he didn't tell you just now was that I got the

lead role in that show and he wound up in the chorus. But John, from that day to this, and for all the days that follow, you will always be my leading man. From this day forward, I will stand by your side. You are the one I will be true to always. Let us make our lives together.

Outline Three

Opening verse of a favorite song, or quote from a book or poem that is particularly meaningful to you as a couple. Continuation of cited material.

Promise or commitment to each other.

Here's an example:

- **Bride**: Grow old along with me!
- **Groom**: The best is yet to be.
- **Bride**: The last of life, for which the first was made.
- **Groom**: Our times are in his hand Who saith, "A whole I planned; Youth shows but half. Trust God; see all, nor be afraid!"
- **Bride**: God bless our love.
- **Groom**: God bless our love.
- **Bride**: John, in this assembly of friends and family, I take you today as my husband. I do this in the certainty of my soul, and knowing that you are my true life partner. I will love you, honor you, and cherish you for the rest of our days, so long as we shall live.
- **Groom**: Kathy, in this assembly of friends and family, I take you today as my wife. I do this in the certainty

of my soul, and knowing that you are my true life partner. I will love you, honor you, and cherish you for the rest of our days, so long as we shall live.

Outline Four

Bride: Dictionary definition of an important aspect of your relationship.
Groom: Elaboration on this theme, extending into your own interpretation, as a couple, of the word or phrase.
Both: Promise or commitment to each other.

- **Bride**: The dictionary defines love as the attraction or affection felt for a person who elicits delight and admiration.
- **Groom**: For us, as we begin our lives together, that definition is only a beginning. We make a commitment to our love today, and we see it as a willingness to give, to see oneself through another, and to work together to make the best parts of ourselves a reality.
- **Bride**: John, my love for you is the foundation upon which I want to build my life. Take this ring as a sign of my faith.
- **Groom**: Kathy, my love for you is the foundation upon which I want to build my life. Take this ring as a sign of my faith.

Outline Five

Groom: Brief statement acknowledging and celebrating the gathering of friends and family.

Bride: Longer statement continuing this idea.
Both: Promise or commitment to each other.

Here's an example:

✿ **Groom**: Today we bring two families together and celebrate as one family.

✿ **Bride**: To all who have come with us to mark our union today, we offer our thanks for your help through the years, our embrace for your support over the weeks and months that led to this day, and our promise that, as new members of this new and larger family, we will always be there for you as you have been there for us.

✿ **Groom**: Kathy, in joining my life with yours, I give you all that I am and all that I may become. I give myself to you as your husband.

✿ **Bride**: John, in joining my life with yours, I give you all that I am and all that I may become. I give myself to you as your wife.

Outline Six

Scriptural passage that is particularly meaningful to you as a couple.
Continuation of cited material.
Promise or commitment to each other.

Here's an example:

✿ **Groom**: From the beginning of creation God made them male and female.

- **Bride**: This is why a man must leave father and mother . . .
- **Groom**: . . . and the two become one body. They are no longer two, therefore, but one body.
- **Bride**: So then, what God has united . . .
- **Groom**: . . . man must not divide.
- **Bride**: John, today, in the gathering of this honored company, we unite in God's love. I pledge myself to you as your wife, and will be faithful to you for all of our days.
- **Groom**: Kathy, today, in the gathering of this honored company, we unite in God's love. I pledge myself to you as your husband, and will be faithful to you for all of our days.

Outline Seven

With your partner, develop a single paragraph to be recited by both of you. The paragraph should draw on the material you have discussed in your premarital counseling.

Here's an example:

- I, John, take you, Kathy, to be my wife. I want to grow old along with you; I want to share the blessings of children and family with you. Today, before these honored guests and beloved family members, I vow to love you and honor you for as long as we both live.

I vow to respect you, listen to you, and grow with you, through good times and bad times.

Ⓔ *Question?*

What is a covenant marriage?
Some couples, like former Arkansas governor and Baptist pastor Mike Huckabee and his wife Janet, have a covenant marriage. This is where a couple agrees to engage in special, religious premarital counseling and can subsequently only divorce under extreme circumstances such as abuse, drug use, conviction of a felony, or other serious offenses. It is legal only in a handful of states.

A Word to the Wise

Stay away from negative imagery. Remember, as John Donne said, "I am two fools, I know, for loving, and for saying so in whining poetry." By all means, express yourself, but keep it light. Your vows should be inspirational and uplifting, not ominous and foreboding. When you start writing, try to think about all the positive qualities that you bring to your marriage. The following example should serve as a marital vow don't:

❧ I, Kathy, take you, John, to be my husband from this day forward. I promise never to stray from the path that we forge as we face our tomorrows together as one. This wedding is a true joining of souls. Although we've had our ups and downs in the past, our lawful union will not outlast the love, trust, and harmony that exist between us today. I promise to be vigilant in preserving these, our shared values, as the mainstays of our marriage no matter what manner of hardship comes our way.

Equally irrelevant are the arguments and breakups that you and your fiancé may have had in the past. Unless you're referring to the time you helped your fiancé through an illness, or something of this nature, mentioning past "ups and downs" is completely uncalled for.

Don't Wait Until the Last Minute

Even if you're an adrenalin junkie who works best under pressure, do yourself a favor and don't leave the vow writing until you're being driven to the church. This exercise requires a clear head and calm demeanor, neither of which you will have right before the wedding.

There are many people who feel that they are most creative when they are under the gun. In the classic *Calvin and Hobbes* comic strip by Bill Watterson, Calvin declares, "You can't just turn on creativity like a faucet. You have to be in the right mood." To which Hobbes asks, "What mood is that?" Calvin replies, "Last-minute panic."

The problem with people who take this approach is that they are only creative when they are forced. These are people who enjoy the thrill of procrastination. Writing your vows requires craft, not adrenalin.

Ⓔ *Question?*

Can I make him promise to mow the lawn every week?
Keep it classy. No one wants or needs to hear about how often you promise to paint the house or be intimate with each other. If you absolutely must put these things on paper, do it in a prenuptial agreement where the only people who will be aghast are your attorneys who are paid to keep quiet.

Start jotting down your thoughts at least several weeks before the wedding, and don't expect to get it perfect the first time. Most professional authors go through several drafts before they're satisfied with their results. You might even want to walk away and let your brain percolate for a bit in order to find the perfect words or phrase. If you're the kind of person who wakes up in the middle of the night with "Eureka!" moments, keep a pad and pencil on your bed table so you can remember your nocturnal brilliance in the morning. If you find yourself in a situation where you can't write something down, you can always call yourself and leave a voicemail. It sounds silly, but it works.

Chapter 3
Finding Inspiration

Writer's block can hit at the most inconvenient times. The following pages contain emergency creativity repair treatments. In all probability, you haven't written a poem since high school, and your e-mails are hammered out in only the most workmanlike of fashions. There's no shame in admitting it, so you might as well 'fess up—your imagination is in a state of hibernation. The sooner you come to grips with this, the quicker you'll snap out of it.

Stop and Smell the Roses

The best time to reconnect with your imagination is on a weekend or a day off from work, when there's nothing to be done but take naps after breakfast, watch *E! True Hollywood Story* marathons, and catch up on the classics of Western literature.

Alert!

We all use our creative thought processes to put out fires on the job and plan outings with friends, but only poets and writers channel their creativity into the written word on a daily basis. Think of your creativity as a muscle. If you haven't stretched it in a while, it may be a little stiff at first, but eventually it will run smoothly.

Pull up a window seat and savor your breakfast coffee without the TV or radio. Take in the architecture, follow the goings on of pedestrians as they mill about your intersection, watch your neighbor's kid mow the lawn. Listen to the sounds around you—the bees buzzing, the birds chirping, the cars honking, the sirens blaring. Whether your aural landscape is a bucolic dream or a big city cacophony, your task is to pay attention and find the beauty in it.

Free Your Brain

This is your time to do whatever you want. You can escape into a dream world wherein you waltz through your wedding day with all the grace of Fred and Ginger, try on every outfit in your closet and prance before the full-length mirror or choreograph a dance routine and commit it to motor memory. If visualizing doesn't work for you, one or more of the following exercises should keep you occupied while shifting your pursuit of imagination into high gear.

Question?

But what if I'm not a creative person?
Everyone's brain is different. Einstein wrote ground-breaking physics papers, but was hard put to figure out a waiter's tip. Even though he was a preeminent scientist, he managed to bang out tender love letters to the many women in his life.

Produce Your Own Blockbuster Soundtrack

Some people are visual learners, others are aural. We all know how a movie's soundtrack can make us feel emotions more intensely than the images on the screen. To break your inspirational logjam, create your own soundtrack of love songs.

Choose songs that focus on love, not sex. Forget about having a good beat; you're not looking for a dance mix, you're looking for inspiration. That may mean listening to songs off your regular play list. Songs from musical theater are inspiring because they tell a story and are often about a special quality of the beloved.

However you fill up your mix, just fill it up. Then let it play as you go about the following exercises. Between the music and the activities, you'll have more inspiration than you'll know what to do with.

Create a Collage

Get out your poster board and draw an outline of you and your fiancé. It doesn't have to be a masterpiece. Now grab scissors and some magazines. Flip through the glossy pages and begin cutting and pasting the images that best represent how you view your relationship at its start, at the present time, and in the future. Don't limit yourself to pictures; if you see certain colors and words that define the stages of your romance, incorporate them as well.

Get Out the Crayons

On a plain white sheet of paper, draw a picture of your dream house. Use colored crayons or pencils and make the walls transparent so you can see inside. Don't try to be realistic; fill the house with whatever you want.

Here's another artistic exercise: Your wedding is a major life-altering event. Can you think of something in nature, be it animal, vegetable, or mineral, that goes through a similar transformation? Go ahead and draw a picture of it, and don't skimp on the colors.

The Great Outdoors

Now that you've been cooped up for hours with nothing but arts and crafts and your imagination to amuse you, you're probably dying to get outside and make some snow angels or sandcastles. Whatever the season, you're never going to find a better time to enjoy all that nature has to offer. You've got two full hours in which to indulge your yen for fresh air.

As you wander, keep your eyes peeled. You've probably traversed the same route on countless occasions, but have you really taken the time to notice all the small things that make your neck of the woods unique? In all likelihood, you're far too busy to concern yourself with such trifles on a daily basis. The following guidelines should start you thinking in the right direction.

Ⓔ Essential

For the best inspiration, look at other couples. See who looks happy and ask yourself why. Look at the lives all around you. Make up stories. What you see will provide fodder for your vows. Jot down simple one- or two-word notes to remind yourself of these images later on.

People and Places

Pretend that you've just learned the meaning of the word *why* and ask away. Why does the sign say "Don't Walk" when there are no cars in sight? Why do the geese come to the man-made pond on the corner every year at this time? Why is that strange man talking to a brown paper bag?

Make up your own answers, with no regard to the laws of urban planning, environmental science, or common sense. Try to give answers that tell a story, and see if your time outside doesn't turn into something quite extraordinary.

While you're out and about, take some time to observe the passersby. Take note of everything from what they're wearing to how they carry themselves. What secrets lurk behind their seemingly placid facial expressions? Where are they going? Where have they been? Every person is a mystery just waiting to be solved, and so is every park bench, street corner, and suburban home. Try to imagine what goes on behind the closed front doors. Consider all the little dramas that might have unfolded at the Washington and Elm intersection. Reflect upon all the romances that might have come alive beneath that hundred-year-old oak tree.

Back at the Drawing Board

Once you're back inside, bask in the comfort of your own four walls. Inspiration waits for no one, so take out a pencil and start writing. Your powers of imagination are now at their peak, so take full advantage of this opportunity. To prepare yourself for the task that lies ahead, you should follow these guidelines to the letter:

- Disconnect your phone, turn off your cell, and put away that pager. The last thing you need when you're in the middle of writing the greatest sentences you've ever written is to hear your friends calling to complain about something.

- Close your door, shut your windows, and drown out the more stubborn noise with the sound of music. The lyrics in the inspiration mix you made before will get in the way of writing, but orchestral soundtracks from great romances could be helpful here.

- Settle in for the long haul. If you sneak off in search of the refrigerator every time words seem to fail you, you're not going to finish the deed before you (or fit into your dress). Stay put until you're satisfied with what you've written. One short break is all you're entitled to, so use it wisely.

- Recall the seven outlines that were listed in Chapter 2. Whether you go back to consult these or devise an original outline of your own, make sure to set up a series of steps that will let you know you're making progress.

- Think positively. If you approach the work with uncertainty and doubt, the vows will suffer. While this is important, it's not astrophysics—you can do it and it is fun.

Last Words of Advice

For the first draft of your wedding vows, you need to get everything out on paper as fast as possible. Free write without thinking or editing to create as much material as you can. Once you've written enough to work with (and only you can be the judge of how much is enough), start editing and shaping your vows. As you begin to apply yourself to editing your vows, do not feel compelled to keep your pencil in perpetual motion. Since editing is about the quality and not the quantity of your writing, thinking will probably take up most of your time. No doubt, you'll also find yourself doing a great deal of research, flipping through the following pages and consulting other texts that you find personally relevant.

Today's Arts and Crafts Projects

If you made a collage, you're a natural storyteller. Pay special attention to the images and words you chose to feature in your project. If you look long enough, you'll find that these tell a special kind of love story, and it just might be one that deserves to be summarized in your vows.

Those who chose to draw a picture should understand that your decision reflects your hopeful and wishful state of mind. Your dreams are important to you, so don't be shy about incorporating these into your wedding vows.

Look at your picture of this morning and consider what it is that you compared your wedding day to. Go with this insight, not only including it in your vows, but also elaborating and building upon it to create a true love poem. As you look at your morning's artwork, note the colors you used and try to connect these to the feelings and emotions you might be experiencing as you approach your wedding day. Again, these might merit inclusion in your vows.

Something Borrowed

William Shakespeare had good reason to warn against borrowing; history has yet to witness a more imposed-upon scribe. But one man's loss is another's gain, so feel free to rifle through this book's lengthy collection of quotes for inspiration. Just one brilliant sentence can open the floodgates to your creative process.

You could also begin by choosing to crib a solitary line, such as Edmund Spenser's "Let baser things devise to lie in dust, but you shall live by fame." From that point on, you can carry on however you like, writing your own heartfelt poem. For instance, "Let baser things devise to lie in dust, but you shall live by fame, for I vow to celebrate your virtues and glorify your name. But, whether toiling in obscurity or renowned throughout, you'll always be the only one whom I can't live without." Have fun, and may the spirit of the occasion move you!

Chapter 4
A Ceremony All Your Own

Writing your own wedding vows is a great beginning, but why stop there? Believe it or not, you can craft the whole ceremony to suit your specifications, provided, of course, that your officiant doesn't have any objections. Retooling the entire ceremony will mean more writing work for you and your partner, but if it means making the proceedings more meaningful, then no effort is too great.

Traditional Weddings

You'd be surprised at just how many couples choose to craft their wedding ceremonies from start to finish. Whether it's due to a desire to break new ground, an aversion to strict formality, a lack of religious beliefs, or a yearning for a more spiritually satisfying ceremony, more and more people are turning tradition on its ear and delighting their wedding guests with something quite unexpected.

To successfully update your wedding ceremony, you need a firm grasp on the various ingredients that go into a standard ceremony. Up to now, much of this book has focused on wedding vows. While these are important, they are by no means the alpha and omega of the wedding service. Most ceremonies break down as follows:

- Introduction/greeting: The officiant greets the guests and calls attention to the solemn nature of marriage and the wedding vows and asks all assembled to respect the union.
- Readings: Poetry, scripture, or other meaningful passages the bride and groom have chosen are read aloud.
- Declaration of consent/intent: These are the so-called "I dos" whereby both partners assert that they enter into the marriage by their own volition.
- Vows: These are the cornerstone of the ceremony, in which the bride and groom address each other and promise to fulfill their roles as husband and wife.
- Ring exchange: The traditional act of exchanging wedding rings is meant to symbolize an eternal union.

- Pronouncement of marriage: The officiant pronounces the bride and groom husband and wife. It is usually followed by a kiss.

Alert!

In most mainstream Western Christian religions, the wedding ceremony has only two mandatory parts: the declarations of intent and the pronouncement of marriage. By including supplementary readings and music, or omitting certain parts of the proceeding altogether, couples can concoct a service that is in keeping with their beliefs, personalities, and lifestyles.

The Sound of Music

Asking your friends to sing and read should add some good old-fashioned fun to the ceremony, but believe it or not, there's still more you can do to ensure that your guests don't drift off while the ceremony is still in full swing. Even the most solemn weddings can benefit from a carefully selected soundtrack. After all, well-chosen music, just like well-chosen words, can provide atmosphere and enhance the mood and meaning of your ceremony from start to finish.

Most couples don't give much thought to ceremony music. With the exception of "Here Comes the Bride," there aren't too many pieces of music that are directly associated with marriage. But these days, more and more couples are spicing up their ceremony with a variety of songs, musicians, and singers. If these are options you'd like to consider, consult with the officiant in charge of your ceremony as soon as possible. Some religions and houses of worship place restrictions on secular selections during the ceremony, so ask about this well in advance.

Ⓔ Alert!

Be careful about asking friends or relatives to perform. In the film *Four Weddings and a Funeral*, a couple sings an awful rendition of "I Can't Live Without You" in front of the altar at the first wedding. You don't want your guests feeling compelled to make rude gestures in the middle of the ceremony like Simon Callow's character Gareth did.

Your best bet for finding appropriate music is to check with the musical coordinator for the ceremony site. Most religious facilities have a staff organist or choir director who can help you choose the best music. The coordinator can also recommend singers and musicians who have performed well at other functions. Don't worry if you think you don't know enough about classical or "church" music; the musicians you choose can offer suggestions based on the guidelines you set forth.

Most ceremony music in a traditional Christian wedding is broken up into four parts: prelude, processional, ceremony, and recessional. For civil ceremonies, there is usually a prelude, processional, and recessional. In addition, there can be music for the signing of the register. Each of these sections has its own function and style. You should choose music that is suitable for each.

Ⓔ Essential

Before you hire a full orchestra to accompany the church choir, remember that the cost of musicians and singers for the ceremony must fit into your budget. It may take some planning, but don't be intimidated—you can have wonderful music for both the ceremony and the reception with a little compromise and ingenuity.

The Prelude

The prelude is the music that plays from the time the guests start arriving until all of them are seated and the mother of the bride is ready to make her entrance. The options for music here are very broad: upbeat, slow, or a mixture of both. You want the prelude to establish a mood as well as entertain the guests while they wait. The end of the prelude, right before the processional, is usually a good time for a soloist or choir to sing a song (during which the mother of the bride would be seated).

The Processional

This is the music that accompanies the wedding party down the aisle. A traditional march helps to set the pace for nervous feet—and carry the spirit of the day toward the altar. When it's time for you to make that long trek down the aisle, you can walk to the same piece as the bridesmaids or to a piece chosen especially for you. Some processional favorites include:

- "Waltz of the Flowers," Tchaikovsky
- "Wedding March," Mendelssohn
- "Bridal Chorus" (Here Comes the Bride), Wagner
- "Trumpet Voluntary," Dupuis
- "Trumpet Voluntary," Clarke
- "Trumpet Tune," Purcell
- "The Dance of the Sugar Plum Fairies," Tchaikovsky
- "Ode to Joy," Beethoven
- "The March," Tchaikovsky
- "Ave Maria," Schubert
- "The Austrian Wedding March" (traditional)
- "Canon in D Major," Pachelbel

The Ceremony

Music that is played during the wedding ceremony itself is called ceremony music. The right music here can enhance the mood and emphasize the meaning of the marriage ceremony. Some ceremony music favorites include:

- "My Tribute," Crouch
- "The Lord's Prayer," Malotte
- "Panis Angelicus," Franck

- "Now Thank We All Our God," Bach
- "Saviour Like a Shepherd Lead Us," Bradbury
- "Cherish the Treasure," Mohr
- "We've Only Just Begun," the Carpenters
- "The Unity Candle Song," Sullivan
- "The Bride's Prayer," Good
- "The Wedding Prayer," Dunlap
- "All I Ask of You," Lloyd Webber
- "Wherever You Go," Callahan
- "The Wedding Song," Stookey
- "The Irish Wedding Song" (traditional)

The Recessional

This is your exit music. The song should be joyous and upbeat, reflecting your happiness at being joined for life to the person accompanying you up the aisle. Some recessional favorites include:

- "The Russian Dance," Tchaikovsky
- "Trumpet Tune," Stanley
- "Toccata Symphony V," Widor
- "All Creatures of Our God and King," Williams
- "Trumpet Fanfare (Rondeau)," Mouret
- "Pomp and Circumstance," Elgar
- "Praise, My Soul, the King of Heaven," Goss
- "Arrival of the Queen of Sheba," Handel

The right music should complement and underscore the spirit of the marriage ceremony and may even help you get to the heart of the matter as you sit down to compose the vows that you will be speaking before your love, your family, and your friends.

Symbols of Love

To further personalize your wedding, you may choose to include a symbolic ceremony. Much like the ring exchange, the wine ceremony and the unity candle-lighting ceremony are beautiful, albeit lesser-known, traditions that may add to your overall marriage ceremony. You might want to consider giving a flower from your bouquet to your mother and new mother-in-law as you walk up the aisle. Or, take your vows by candlelight and have the church bells ring as you are declared husband and wife. Other wedding ceremony elements include glass breaking, hand blessing, handfasting, red rose exchange, sand blending, and white dove release.

Check with your officiant before undertaking any less conventional plan of action, but always remember that this is your wedding!

Chapter 5
The Classic Vows

If you're still stuck for inspiration, you can always review the wedding vows from some of the world's largest religions. You may decide to use them as a framework, or you may decide writing your own vows is not necessary when a group of elderly bearded men have already come up with the perfect words. In any event, they make for some mighty interesting reading. Bear in mind that most religions have different branches that may advocate different wordings. The following are middle-of-the-road versions of some religions' marriage vows.

Western Christian Religions

Many of these religions' vows have very similar wording. You've probably heard them a thousand times, but they never grow old. They're classics for a reason.

Baptist

There are many different branches of Baptist churches, and they can have some very different rules regarding whom they will and will not marry. Some will refuse to marry couples who are living together or who do not claim to have been "born again in Jesus Christ." Check with your pastor about the restrictions within your church.

- Will you, _____, have _____ to be your wife/husband? Will you love her/him, comfort and keep her/him, and forsaking all other remain true to her/him as long as you both shall live?
- I will.
- With this ring I thee wed, and all my worldly goods I thee endow. In sickness and in health, in poverty or in wealth, till death do us part.

Episcopalian

For all its stuffy reputation, the Episcopal Church only requires that at least one of the partners be a baptized Christian, and not even necessarily within the denomination. The ceremony must be witnessed by at least two people, conform to the laws of the state and the church, and be presided over by a bishop, priest, or (in some cases) a deacon.

❧ In the name of God, I, _____, take you _____, to be my wife/husband, to have and to hold from this day forward, for better for worse, for richer for poorer, in sickness and in health, to love and to cherish, until we are parted by death. This is my solemn vow.

Latter Day Saints

In LDS wedding ceremonies, neither the bride nor the groom craft their own vows. Instead, the officiator asks the couple if they will agree to the promises of the marriage ceremony and then blesses their union.

❧ Brother/Sister _____, do you take Sister/Brother _____ by the right hand and receive her/him unto yourself to be your lawful and wedded wife/husband for time and all eternity, with a covenant and promise that you will observe and keep all the laws, rites, and ordinances pertaining to this Holy Order of Matrimony in the New and Everlasting Covenant, and this you do in the presence of God, angels, and these witnesses of your own free will and choice?

Lutheran

Lutheran couples are encouraged to write their own vows with help from their pastor. Lutheran vows stress the commitment to faithfulness, God's faithfulness toward His people, and the community's and couple's commitments of faithfulness to each other.

❧ I, _____, take you, _____ to be my wife/husband, and these things I promise you: I will be faithful to you and honest with you; I will respect, trust, help, and care for you; I will share my life with you; I will forgive you as we have been forgiven; and I will try with you better to understand ourselves, the world, and God; through the best and the worst of what is to come as long as we live.

Methodist

Methodist weddings are viewed as the bringing together of a new family unit within the family of God. Above all, they are spiritual occasions.

❧ Will you have this man/woman to be your husband/wife, to live together in a holy marriage? Will you love him/her, comfort him/her, honor and keep him/her in sickness and in health, and forsaking all others, be faithful to him/her as long as you both shall live?

Religious Society of Friends (Quaker)

Quaker weddings are similar to their weekly Meeting for Worship. The congregation comes together to sit in silence. Anyone (Quaker or not) who is moved to rise and speak is welcome to do so. During the Meeting the couple will stand up, join hands, and say to each other:

❦ In the presence of God and these, our Friends, I
_____ take thee _____ to be my wife/husband,
promising with Divine assistance to be unto thee a
loving and faithful wife/husband as long as we both
shall live.

After the Meeting is over, every witness is asked to sign the
wedding document.

Roman Catholic

As with most other denominations, there are both liberal and conservative parishes in the United States, and
the exact wording and amount of vow tinkering allowed
will depend on the priest in charge.

❦ I, _____, take you, _____, to be my husband/wife.
I promise to be true to you in good times and in bad,
in sickness and in health. I will love and honor you all
the days of my life.

Orthodox Christian Religions

Traditionally, most Orthodox religions do not require
public vows from the couple. It is assumed that they
already have an understanding with each other. As
such, many of these churches' wedding ceremonies are
set in stone with little room for originality. But it's still
worth asking your priest if you can include some of your
own sentiments.

Greek Orthodox

Greek Orthodox marriage does not unite a couple. Its role is to recognize a union that God has already made. Thus, marriage is more than a legal contract. There are no vows because the man and woman are assumed to have already committed to one another and welcomed God's presence in their marriage. There is no "till death do us part." Christ destroyed death by His resurrection. Ergo, the union of the man and woman in Christ is eternal.

Russian Orthodox

In the Russian tradition, vows can be spoken aloud.

❦ I, _____, take you, _____, as my wedded wife/husband and I promise you love, honor, and respect; to be faithful to you, and not to forsake you until death do us part. So help me God, one in the Holy Trinity, and all the saints.

Eastern Religions

There are too many different religions in the world to count, but the oldest and among the most venerated come from the Middle East and Far East.

Buddhist

Because marriages are viewed as strictly secular affairs, Buddhist weddings are not presided over by a priest or monk, although many couples will seek a religious blessing before their ceremony. Typical elements of a Buddhist wedding may include ancestor worship, the lighting of candles and incense, the bestowing of gifts, chanting, and a recitation of the traditional marital expectations according to the Sigalovada Sutta:

- **Officiant**: In five ways should a wife, as Western quarter, be ministered to by her husband: by respect, by courtesy, by faithfulness, by handing over authority to her, by providing her with ornaments. In these five ways does the wife minister to by her husband as the Western quarter, love him: her duties are well-performed by hospitality to kin of both, by faithfulness, by watching over the goods he brings and by skill and industry in discharging all business.
- **Groom**: Towards my wife I undertake to love and respect her, be kind and considerate, be faithful, delegate domestic management, provide gifts to please her.
- **Bride**: Towards my husband I undertake to perform my household duties efficiently, be hospitable to my in-laws and friends of my husband, be faithful, protect and invest our earnings, discharge my responsibilities lovingly and conscientiously.

Hindu

Hindu wedding vows are quite strict, involving the Seven Steps.

- Let us take the first steps to provide for our household a nourishing and pure diet, avoiding those foods injurious to healthy living. Let us take the second step to develop physical, mental, and spiritual powers. Let us take the third step, to increase our wealth by righteous means and proper use. Let us take the fourth step to acquire knowledge, happiness, and harmony by mutual love and trust. Let us take the fifth step, so that we be blessed with strong, virtuous, and heroic children. Let us take the sixth step, for self-restraint and longevity. Finally, let us take the seventh step and be true companions and remain lifelong partners by this wedlock.

❀ We have taken the Seven Steps. You have become mine forever. Yes, we have become partners. I have become yours. Hereafter, I cannot live without you. Do not live without me. Let us share the joys. We are word and meaning, united. You are thought and I am sound. May the night be honey-sweet for us; may the morning be honey-sweet for us; may the earth be honey-sweet for us and the heavens be honey-sweet for us. May the plants be honey-sweet for us; may the sun be all honey for us; may the cows yield us honey-sweet milk. As the heavens are stable, as the earth is stable, as the mountains are stable, as the whole universe is stable, so may our unions be permanently settled.

Islamic

Most Muslim couples do not recite vows, but rather listen to the words of the imam. He imparts thoughts about what marriage means and what the couple's responsibilities are to each other and to Allah. Afterward, they agree to become husband and wife and are blessed by the congregation.

Occasionally, some Muslim brides and grooms will choose to recite vows.

- **Bride**: I, _____, offer you myself in marriage in accordance with the instructions of the Holy Quran and the Holy Prophet, peace and blessing be upon Him. I pledge, in honesty and with sincerity, to be for you an obedient and faithful wife.
- **Groom**: I pledge, in honesty and sincerity, to be for you a faithful and helpful husband.

Jewish

The act of consecration is accomplished by the giving of a ring (or another article of some value) by the man to the woman. The only words spoken by the couple during a Jewish ceremony come when the groom puts the ring on the bride's finger. He says, "You are betrothed to me with this ring according to the law of Moses and Israel." The speaking is merely to clarify what his intentions are with the gift. Vows are not really the binding factors.

If the bride wishes to give her husband a wedding ring, it is traditionally done at a different time. The ring is a symbolic gift the groom gives his bride, and the bride is not supposed to give the groom anything in exchange. However, many couples today opt for double ring ceremonies with vows.

Jewish couples sign a *ketubah*, which spells out the groom's responsibilities to the bride. After that the groom lifts the bride's veil to ensure that he is marrying the girl of his choice (after all, he doesn't want his father-in-law to pull a fast one like the Old Testament's Laban did to poor Jacob and Rachel). The couple is married under a canopy called a *chuppah*, which represents God's protection.

Scriptural Passages

Biblical passages are an inspired choice for your vows. The following is a selection of some of the most popular for you to choose from.

And God blessed them, and God said to them, Be fruitful and multiply, and fill the earth and subdue it.

—**Genesis 1:28**

How much better is thy love than wine!

—**Song of Solomon 4:10**

And the Lord God said, It is not good that the man should be alone; I will make him a help meet for him. And out of the ground, the Lord God formed every beast of the field, and every fowl of the air; and brought them unto Adam to see what he would call them: and whatsoever Adam called every living creature, that was the name thereof. And Adam gave names to all cattle, and to the fowl of the air, and to every beast of the field; but for Adam there was not found a help meet for him. And the Lord caused a deep sleep to fall upon Adam, and he slept: and he took one of his ribs, and closed up the flesh instead thereof; and the rib, which the Lord God had taken from the man, made he a woman, and brought her unto the man. And Adam said, This is now bone of my bones, and flesh of my flesh: she shall be called Woman, because she was taken out of Man. Therefore shall a man leave his father and his mother, and shall cleave unto his wife; and they shall be one flesh.

—**Genesis 2:18–24**

From the beginning of creation God made them male and female. For this cause shall a man leave his father and mother, and cleave to his wife; and they twain shall be one flesh: so then they are no more twain, but one flesh. What therefore God hath joined together, let not man put asunder.

—**Mark 10:6–9**

As the Father hath loved me, so have I loved you: continue ye in my love. If ye keep my commandments, ye shall abide in love; even as I have kept my Father's commandments, and abide in his love. These things have I spoken unto you, that my joy might remain in you, and that your joy might be full. This is my commandment: that ye love one another as I have loved you.

—**John 15:9–12**

Walk in love, as Christ also hath loved us, and hath given himself for us as an offering and a sacrifice to God for a sweet-smelling savor.

—**Ephesians 5:2**

Blessed is every one that feareth the Lord; that walketh in his ways. For thou shalt eat the labor of thine hands; happy shalt thou be, and it shall be well with thee. Thy wife shall be as a fruitful vine by the sides of thine house, thy children like olive plants around thy table. Behold, that thus shall the man be blessed that feareth the Lord.

—**Psalm 128:1–4**

He brought me to the banqueting house, and his banner over me was love.

—**Song of Solomon 2:4**

Whither thou goest, I will go; and where thou lodgest, I will lodge; thy people shall be my people, and thy God, my God. Where thou diest, will I die, and there will I be buried.

—**Ruth 1:16–17**

Many waters cannot quench love, neither can the floods drown it.

—**Song of Solomon 8:7**

Love is patient; love is kind and envies no one. Love is never boastful, nor conceited, nor rude; never selfish, not quick to take offense. Love keeps no score of wrongs; does not gloat over other men's sins, but delights in the truth. There is nothing love cannot face; there is no limit to its faith, its hope, and its endurance.

—**1 Corinthians 13:4–7**

My beloved spake, and said unto me, Rise up, my love, my fair one, and come away.

—**Song of Solomon 2:10**

Make a joyful noise unto the Lord, all ye lands. Serve the Lord with gladness: come before his presence with singing.

Know ye that the Lord he is God: it is he that hath made us, and not we ourselves; we are his people, and the sheep of his pasture. Enter into his gates with thanksgiving, and into his courts with praise: be thankful unto him, and bless his name. For the Lord is good, his mercy is everlasting; and his truth endureth to all generations.

—Psalm 100

Husbands ought to love their wives as their own bodies. He who loves his wife loves himself.

—Ephesians 5:25–26

Love . . . binds everything together in perfect harmony.
—Colossians 3:14

I have found the one whom my soul loves.
—Song of Solomon 3:4

There is no fear in love, but perfect love casts out fear.
—1 John 4:18

He who does not love does not know God; for God is love.
—1 John 4:8

Two are better than one because they have a good reward for their labor. For if they fall, one will lift up his companion. But woe to him who is alone when he falls, for he has no one to help lift him up.

—Ecclesiastes 4:9–10

May the love you share be as timeless as the tides and as deep as the sea.

—1 Corinthians 13

When a man is newly married, he shall not go out with the army or be charged with any business; he shall be free at home one year, to be happy with his wife whom he has taken.

—Deuteronomy 24:5

Let him kiss me with the kisses of his mouth: for thy love is better than wine.

—Song of Solomon 1:2

And now abide faith, hope, love, these three; but the greatest of these is love.

—1 Corinthians 13:13

Let us not love in word, neither in tongue; but in deed and in truth.

—1 John 3:18

True love is the absence of fear.

—1 John 4:18

As the lily among thorns, so is my love among the daughters. As the apple tree among the trees of the wood, so is my beloved among the sons. I sat down under his shadow with great delight, and his fruit was sweet to my taste.

—Song of Solomon 2:2–3

I may be able to speak the languages of human beings and even of angels, but if I have no love, my speech is no more than a noisy gong or a clanging bell. I may have the gift of inspired preaching; I may have all knowledge and understand all secrets; I may have the faith needed to move mountains—but if I have no love, I am nothing. I may give away everything I have, and even give up my body to be burned—but if I have no love, this does me no good.

—1 Corinthians 13:1–13

Above all else, guard thy heart for it is the wellspring of life.

—Proverbs 4:23

Come let us take our fill of love until the morning: let us solace ourselves with love.

—Proverbs 7:18

Other Religious Traditions

Many other religious traditions have thought-provoking ideas that might appeal to you and your affianced.

When two people are at one in their inmost hearts, they shatter even the strength of iron or of bronze.

—the *I Ching*

Blessed art thou, O Lord, King of the Universe, who created mirth and joy, bridegroom and bride, gladness, jubilation, dancing, and delight, love and brotherhood, peace and fellowship. Quickly, O, Lord our God, may the sound of mirth and joy be heard in the streets of Judah and Jerusalem, the voice of bridegroom and bride, jubilant voices of bridegrooms from their canopies and youths from the feasts of song. Blessed art thou, O Lord, who makes the bridegroom rejoice with the bride.

—the Talmud (Ketubot 8[a])

When love is strong, a man and woman can make their bed on a sword's blade. When love grows weak, a bed of 60 cubits is not large enough.

—**the Talmud**

Only the complete person can love.

—**Confucius**

Sweet be the glances we exchange, our faces showing true concord. Enshrine me in thy heart, and let a single spirit dwell within us.

—**Atharva-Veda**

I am He, you are She; I am Song, you are Verse; I am Heaven, you are Earth. Together shall we dwell here, becoming parents of children.

—**Atharva-Veda**

The moral man will find the moral law beginning in the relation between husband and wife, but ending only in the vast reaches of the universe.

—**Confucius**

When the one man loves the one woman and the one woman loves the one man, the very angels desert heaven and sit in that house and sing for joy.

—**Braham-Sutra**

Chapter 6
Great Verses of Love

In this chapter, you will find excerpts from some of the greatest poems relating to love and marriage. You may wish to use one or more of these excerpts as a starting point for developing your own vows. Alternatively, you may decide to use a quote as a supplementary reading during your wedding ceremony. These are some of the most moving words ever penned, so sit back in front of a roaring fire and read some of these verses aloud to each other. They will move and inspire you.

I am not sure that Earth is round
Nor that the sky is really blue.
The tale of why the apples fall
May or may not be true.
I do not know what makes the tides
Nor what tomorrow's world may do,
But I have certainty enough,
For I am sure of you.

—**Amelia Josephine Burr**

Drink to me only with thine eyes,
And I will pledge with mine;
Or leave a kiss but in the cup,
And I'll not look for wine.
The thirst that from the soul doth rise
Doth ask a drink divine;
But might I of Jove's nectar sup,
I would not change for thine.

—**Ben Jonson**

. . . true love is a durable fire,
In the mind ever burning,
Never sick, never old, never dead,
From itself never turning.

—**Sir Walter Raleigh**

They sin who tell us love can die;
With life all other passions fly,
All others are but vanity.

—**Robert Southey**

. . . come the wild weather, come sleet or come snow,
We will stand by each other, however it blow.

—Simon Dach

We loved with a love that was more than a love.

—Edgar Allan Poe

Thou art the star that guides me
Along life's changing sea;
And whate'er fate betides me,
This heart still turns to thee.

—George P. Morris

You know you're in love when you can't fall asleep because
reality is finally better than your dreams.

Theodor Seuss Geisel (Dr. Seuss)

Now the rite is duly done,
Now the word is spoken,
And the spell has made us one
Which may ne'er be broken.

—Winthrop Mackworth Praed

My fellow, my companion, held most dear,
My soul, my other self, my inward friend.

—Mary Sidney Herbert

Flesh of my flesh, bone of my bone, I here, though there, yet
both but one.

—Anne Bradstreet

Fact

> Anne Bradstreet was very well educated for an English girl in the seventeenth century. She married her sweetheart at age sixteen and emigrated to the American colonies with her husband and parents. In her poetry she quietly and sometimes humorously railed against the Puritan strictures placed on her sex.

Each shining light above us
Has its own peculiar grace;
But every light of heaven
Is in my darling's face.

—**John Hay**

Those worlds, for which the conqueror sighs,
For me would have no charms:
My only world thy gentle eyes—
My throne thy circling arms!
Oh, yes, so well, so tenderly
Thou'rt loved, adored by me,
Whole realms of light and liberty
Were worthless without thee.

—**Thomas Moore**

I think true love is never blind,
But rather brings an added light,
An inner vision quick to find
The beauties hid from common sight.
No soul can ever clearly see

Another's highest, noblest part,
Save through the sweet philosophy
And loving wisdom of the heart.

—**Phoebe Cary**

Love is not getting, but giving;
It is goodness, and honor, and peace and pure living.
—**Henry Van Dyke**

Were you the earth, dear Love, and I the skies,
My love should shine on you like to the sun,
And look upon you with ten thousand eyes
Till heaven wax'd blind, and till the world were done.

—**Joshua Sylvester**

The violet loves a sunny bank,
The cowslip loves the lea,
The scarlet creeper loves the elm,
But I love—thee.
The sunshine kisses mount and vale,
The stars they kiss the sea,
The west winds kiss the clover bloom,
But I kiss—thee.
The oriole weds his mottled mate,
The lily's bride o the bee;
Heaven's marriage ring is round the earth,
—Shall I wed thee?

—**Bayard Taylor**

Young bride—a wreath for thee,
Of sweet and gentle flowers;
For wedded love was pure and free
In Eden's happy bowers.
Young bride—a song for thee,
A song of joyous measure,
For thy cup of hope shall be
Filled with honeyed pleasure. . . .
Young bride—a prayer for thee,
That all thy hopes possessing,
Thy soul may praise her God and he
May crown thee with His blessing.

—**Martin Farquhar Tupper**

How much do I love thee?
Go ask the deep sea
How many rare gems
In its coral caves be;
Or ask the broad billows,
That ceaselessly roar,
How many bright sands
Do they kiss on the shore?

—**Mary Ashley Townsend**

I'll love him more, more
Than e'er wife loved before,
Be the days dark or bright.

—**Jean Ingelow**

ⓔ *Fact*

Jean Ingelow was a very popular nineteenth-century English writer. She found great success with her poems and moved to London. Being of a charitable bent, she gave what she called "copyright dinners" three times a week where she invited recently discharged hospital patients to a hearty meal, courtesy of the proceeds of her books.

Only a life lived for another is worthwhile.

—Albert Einstein

There is no surprise more magical than the surprise of being loved: It is God's finger on man's shoulder.

—Charles Morgan

Love is that splendid triggering of human vitality . . . the supreme activity which nature affords anyone for going out of himself towards someone else.

—José Ortega y Gasset

I would like to have engraved inside every wedding band: Be kind to one another. This is the Golden Rule of marriage and the secret of making love last through the years.

—Randolph Ray

Love does not consist of gazing at each other, but in looking outward together in the same direction.

—Antoine de Saint Exupéry

My greatest good fortune in a life of brilliant experiences has been to find you, and to lead my life with you. I don't feel far away from you out here at all. I feel very near in my heart; and also I feel that the nearer I get to honour, the nearer I am to you.

—Winston Churchill, in a letter to his wife, Clementine

Where there is great love there are always miracles.

—Willa Cather

Marriage is not a union merely between two creatures—it is a union between two spirits; and the intention of that bond is to perfect the nature of both.

—Frederick William Robertson

Love, indeed, lends a precious seeing to the eye, and hearing to the ear: all sights and sounds are glorified by the light of its presence.

—Frederick Saunders

When you love someone, you love the whole person, just as he or she is, and not as you would like them to be.

—Leo Tolstoy

Your embraces alone give life to my heart.

—Ancient Egyptian inscription

Love to faults is always blind,
Always is to joy inclin'd,
Lawless, wing'd, and unconfin'd,
And breaks all chains from every mind.

—William Blake

Come live with me and be my love,
And we will all the pleasures prove,
That hills and valleys, dales and fields,
Woods or craggy mountains yield.

—Christopher Marlowe

I know not if I know what true love is,
But if I know, then, if I love not him,
I know there is none other I can love.

—Alfred, Lord Tennyson

Life with its myriad grasp
Our yearning souls shall clasp
By ceaseless love and still expectant wonder;
In bonds that shall endure
Indissolubly sure
Till God in death shall part our paths asunder.

—Arthur Penrhyn Stanley

Teacher, tender comrade, wife,
A fellow-farer true through life.

—Robert Louis Stevenson

If ever two were one, then surely we. If ever man were
loved by wife, then thee.

—Anne Bradstreet

Then Almitra spoke again and said, And what of Marriage,
Master?
And he answered saying:
You were born together, and together you shall be
forevermore.

*You shall be together when the white wings of death scatter
your days.*
Ay, you shall be together even in the silent memory of God.
But let there be spaces in your togetherness,
And let the winds of the heavens dance between you.
Love one another, but make not a bond of love:
*Let it rather be a moving sea between the shores of your
souls.*
Fill each other's cup but drink not from one cup.
*Give one another of your bread but eat not from the same
loaf.*
*Sing and dance together and be joyous, but let each one of
you be alone,*
*Even as the strings of a lute are alone though they quiver
with the same music.*
Give your hearts, but not into each other's keeping.
For only the hand of Life can contain your hearts.
And stand together yet not too near together:
For the pillars of the temple stand apart,
*And the oak tree and the cypress grow not in each other's
shadow.*

—Kahlil Gibran

Life without love is like a tree without blossoms or fruit.

—Kahlil Gibran

It is the heart and not the brain
That to the highest doth attain,
And he who followeth Love's behest
Far excelleth all the rest.

—Henry Wadsworth Longfellow

🄴 *Fact*

A prominent artist and writer, Kahlil Gibran moved to south Boston from what is now Lebanon in 1895 when he was twelve years old. After his mother and two siblings died, he was supported by an older sister and was able to go to art school and then return to Lebanon for college. He never married but maintained intimate friendships with educated and accomplished women.

Had I the heaven's embroidered cloths,
Enwrought with golden and silver light,
The blue and the dim of the dark cloths
Of night and light and the half-light,
I would spread the cloths under your feet:
But I being poor have only my dreams;
I have spread my dreams under your feet;
Tread softly, because you tread on my dreams.

—**William Butler Yeats**

I could not tell fact from fiction
Or if my dream was true
The only sure prediction
In this whole world was you . . .

—**Maya Angelou**

Hope is a thing with feathers
That perches in the soul
And sings a tune without words
And never stops at all.

And sweetest, in the gale, is heard
And sore must be the storm
That could abash the little bird
That keeps so many warm.
I've heard it in the chilliest land
And on the strangest sea
Yet, never, in extremity
It ask a crumb of me.

—**Emily Dickinson**

Somewhere I have never traveled,
Gladly beyond any experience,
Your eyes have their silence:
Something in me understands
The voice of your eyes is deeper than all.

—**e. e. cummings**

And if I can't be with you I would rather have a different
face
And if I can't be near you I would rather be adrift in space
And if the gods desert us I would burn this chapel into
flames
And if someone tries to hurt you I would put myself in your
place.

—**Neil Finn**

What is there in the vale of life
Half so delightful as a wife,
When friendship, love, and peace combine
To stamp the marriage bond divine?

—**William Cowper**

Stone walls do not a prison make,
Nor iron bars a cage;
Minds innocent and quiet take
That for an hermitage;
If I have freedom in my love,
And in my soul am free,
Angels alone that soar above,
Enjoy such liberty.

—**Richard Lovelace**

There has fallen a splendid tear
From the passion-flower by the gate.
She is comming, my dove, my dear;
She is comming, my life, my fate;
The red rose cries, "She is near, she is near,"
And the white rose weeps, "She is late,"
The larkspur listens, "I hear, I hear,"
And the lily whispers, "I wait."

—**Alfred, Lord Tennyson**

Love seeketh not Itself to please,
Nor for itself hath any care;
But for another gives its ease,
And builds a Heaven in Hell's despair.

—**William Blake**

All thoughts, all passions, all delights,
Whatever stirs this mortal frame,
All are but ministers of Love,
And feed his sacred flame.

—**Samuel Taylor Coleridge**

your slightest look easily will unclose me
though i have closed myself as fingers,
you open always petal by petal myself as Spring opens
(touching skillfully, mysteriously) her first rose

—e. e. cummings

Fact

Best known for his playful punctuation, e.e. cummings was a Harvard-educated twentieth-century American poet who was born in Cambridge, Massachusetts. His work makes the most sense when read aloud, rather than silently.

But to see her was to love her, love but her, and love her forever.

—Robert Burns

Look not in my eyes, for fear
They mirror true the sight I see,
And there you find your face too clear
And love it and be lost like me.

—A. E. Housman

Thou wert my joy in every spot,
My theme in every song.
And when I saw a stranger face
Where beauty held the claim,
I gave it like a secret grace
The being of thy name.

And all the charms of face or voice
Which I in others see
Are but the recollected choice
Of what I felt for thee.

—**John Clare**

What love is, if thou wouldst be taught,
Thy heart must teach alone—
Two souls with but a single thought,
Two hearts that beat as one.

—**Friedrich Halm**

Just because I loves you—
That's de reason why
Ma soul is full of color
Like da wings of a butterfly
Just because I loves you
That's de reason why
My heart's a fluttering aspen leaf
When you pass by.

—**Langston Hughes**

Fame, wealth and honor! what are you to Love?

—**Alexander Pope**

Were I as base as is the lowly plain,
And you, my Love, as high as heaven above,
Yet should the thoughts of me your humble swain
Ascend to heaven, in honour of my Love.
Were I as high as heaven above the plain,
And you, my Love, as humble and as low
As are the deepest bottoms of the main,

Whereso'er you were, with you my love should go.
Were you the earth, dear Love, and I the skies,
My love should shine on you like to the sun,
And look upon you with ten thousand eyes
Till heaven wax'd blind, and till the world were done.
Whereso'er I am, below, or else above you,
Whereso'er you are, my heart shall truly love you.

—Samuel Daniel

We cannot kindle when we will
The fire which in the heart resides,
The spirit bloweth and is still,
In mystery our soul abides.

—Matthew Arnold

Our State cannot be severed, we are one,
One Flesh; to lose thee were to lose my self.

—John Milton

So shall a friendship fill each heart
With perfume sweet as roses are,
That even though we be apart,
We'll scent the fragrance from afar.

—Georgia McCoy

Unable are the Loved to die
For Love is Immortality.

—Emily Dickinson

Now you will feel no rain,
For each of you will be shelter to the other.
Now you will feel no cold,

For each of you will be warmth to the other.
Now there is no more loneliness for you,
For each of you will be companion to the other.
Now you are two bodies,
But there is only one life before you.
Go now to your dwelling place,
To enter into the days of your togetherness.
And may your days be good, and long upon the earth.

—Apache blessing

If a thing loves, it is infinite.

—William Blake

Kisses are better fate than wisdom.

—e. e. cummings

That old miracle—Love-at-first-sight—
Needs no explanations. The heart reads aright
Its destiny sometimes.

—Owen Meredith

Sometimes your nearness takes my breath away; and all
the things I want to say can find no voice. Then, in silence,
I can only hope my eyes will speak my heart.

—Robert Sexton

The first sound in the song of love!
Scarce more than silence is, and yet a sound.
Hands of invisible spirits touch the strings
Of the mysterious instrument, the soul,
And play the prelude of our fate.

—Henry Wadsworth Longfellow

O, thou art fairer than the evening air clad in the beauty of a thousand stars.

—Christopher Marlowe

I sought for Love
But Love ran away from me.
I sought my Soul
But my Soul I couldn't see.
Then I sought You,
And I found all three.

—Unknown

Love is a great beautifier.

—Louisa May Alcott

Of all the earthly music, that which reaches farthest into heaven is the beating of a truly loving heart.

—Henry Ward Beecher

Love is just friendship set to music.

—E. Joseph Crossman

It is a good thing to be rich and strong, but it is a better thing to be loved.

—Euripides

Those who love deeply never grow old. They may die of old age, but they die young.

—Benjamin Franklin

It isn't possible to love and to part.

—E. M. Forster

It was a violent case of mutual love at first sight, though neither party was aware of the fact.

—**Mark Twain**

Love is a game that two can play and both can win.

—**Eva Gabor**

Fact

Though he married twice, the fourth-century B.C. Greek playwright Euripides was lucky in neither love nor life. His first wife openly cheated, and his peers mocked him for it (and for being a bit socially backward). His death could hardly have been more dramatic if he had written it for a play. He was allegedly torn apart by dogs belonging to his patron and protector, the king of Macedonia.

No distance of place or lapse of time can lessen the love of those who are thoroughly persuaded of each other's worth.

—**Robert Southey**

Life is the flower for which love is the honey.

—**Victor Hugo**

To love one who loves you,
To admire one who admires you,
In a word, to be the idol of one's idol,
Is exceeding the limit of human joy;

It is stealing fire from heaven.

—**Delphine de Girardin**

Any couple's dream, wished with the same strength, will come true.

—**Susan Polis Schutz**

What counts in making a happy marriage is not so much how compatible you are, but how you deal with incompatibility.

—**George Levinger**

In loving, you lean on someone to hold them up.

—**Rod McKuen**

Age does not protect you from love. But love, to some extent, protects you from age.

—**Jeanne Moreau**

Love is like a wild rose, beautiful and calm, but willing to draw blood in its defense.

—**Mark A. Overby**

To love is to receive a glimpse of heaven.

—**Karen Sunde**

Where love is, there is God also.

—**Leo Tolstoy**

Where there is love there is life.

—**Mahatma Gandhi**

I like not only to be loved, but to be told I am loved.

—**George Eliot**

True love doesn't have a happy ending: true love doesn't have an ending.

—**Unknown**

Love is an act of endless forgiveness, a tender look which becomes a habit.

—**Peter Ustinov**

What I feel for you seems less of earth and more of a cloudless heaven.

—**Victor Hugo**

The power of a glance has been so much abused in love stories, that it has come to be disbelieved in. Few people dare now to say that two beings have fallen in love because they have looked at each other. Yet it is in this way that love begins, and in this way only. The rest is only the rest, and comes afterwards. Nothing is more real than these great shocks which two souls give each other in exchanging this spark.

—**Victor Hugo**

Let my love, like sunshine, surround you, and illuminate your freedom.

—**Rabindranath Tagore**

We are shaped and fashioned by what we love.

—**Johann Wolfgang von Goethe**

The hours I spend with you I look upon as sort of a perfumed garden, a dim twilight, and a fountain singing to it . . . you and you alone make me feel that I am alive. . . .

Other men it is said have seen angels, but I have seen thee and thou art enough.

—**George Moore**

The way you let your hand rest in mine, my bewitching Sweetheart, fills me with happiness. It is the perfection of confiding love. Everything you do, the little unconscious things in particular, charms me and increases my sense of nearness to you, identification with you, till my heart is full to overflowing.

—**Woodrow Wilson**

Your words are my food, your breath my wine. You are everything to me.

—**Sarah Bernhardt**

E *Fact*

Sarah Bernhardt was a nineteenth-century French actress who took the world by storm with her beautiful voice and talent. She left a long line of broken hearts behind her, including that of King Edward VII of England. Even after she lost a leg in her old age, she continued to pack houses by acting from the comfort of an onstage sofa.

I cannot exist without you—I am forgetful of every thing but seeing you again—my Life seems to stop there—I see no further. You have absorb'd me. I have a sensation at the present moment as though I were dissolving. . . . I have been astonished that Men could die Martyrs for religion—I have shudder'd at it—I shudder no more—I could be martyr'd for my Religion—Love is my religion—I could die for that—I could die for you. My creed is Love and you are its only tenet—You have ravish'd me away by a Power I cannot resist.

—**John Keats**

In dreams and in love there are no impossibilities.

—**János Arany**

It is only with the heart that one can see rightly. What is essential is invisible to the eye.

—**Antoine de Saint Exupéry**

This is the miracle that happens every time to those who really love; the more they give, the more they possess.

—**Rainer Maria Rilke**

To love is to place our happiness in the happiness of another.

—**Gottfried Wilhelm von Leibniz**

I have no desire to move mountains, construct monuments, or leave behind in my wake material evidence of my existence. But in the final recollection, if the essence of my being has caused a smile to have appeared upon your face or a touch of joy within your heart, then in living, I have made my mark.

—**Thomas L. Odem Jr.**

One word frees us of all the weight and pain of life: that word is love.

—**Sophocles**

I came alive when I started loving you.

—**C. S. Lewis**

True love doesn't consist of holding hands, it consists of holding hearts.

—**O. A. Battista**

I never knew how to worship until I knew how to love.

—**Henry Ward Beecher**

Love rules the court, the camp, the grove, And men below, and saints above: For love is heaven, and heaven is love.

—**Walter Scott**

Love . . . includes fellowship in suffering, in joy, and in effort.

—**Albert Schweitzer**

Sometimes the heart sees what is invisible to the eye.

—**H. Jackson Brown Jr.**

Listen to no one who tells you how to love. Your love is like no other, and that is what makes it beautiful. Your self is your divinity. . . . Express yourself.

—**Paul Williams**

The greatest happiness of life is the conviction that we are loved—loved for ourselves, or rather, loved in spite of ourselves.

—**Victor Hugo**

To fall in love is easy, even to remain in it is not difficult; our human loneliness is cause enough. But it is a hard quest worth making to find a comrade through whose steady presence one becomes steadily the person one desires to be.

—**Anna Louise Strong**

The moment you have in your heart this extraordinary thing called love and feel the depth, the delight, the ecstasy of it, you will discover that for you the world is transformed.

—**J. Krishnamurti**

Love has nothing to do with what you are expecting to get, it's what you are expected to give—which is everything.

—**Unknown**

Immature love says: "I love you because I need you." Mature love says: "I need you because I love you."

—**Erich Fromm**

The art of love . . . is largely the art of persistence.

—**Albert Ellis**

The hardest of all is learning to be a well of affection, and not a fountain; to show them we love them not when we feel like it, but when they do.

—**Nan Fairbrother**

Love takes off masks that we fear we cannot live without and know we cannot live within.

—**James Baldwin**

The cure for all ills and wrongs, the cares, the sorrows and the crimes of humanity, all lie in the one word "love." It is the divine vitality that everywhere produces and restores life.

—**Lydia Maria Child**

The best proof of love is trust.

—**Joyce Brothers**

 Fact

Dr. Joyce Brothers is an American psychologist and writer who is admired for her compassionate and pragmatic approach to life and its problems. She has had a successful career in radio and television and was one of the first to use the call-in method to offer her listeners and viewers help.

For it was not into my ear you whispered, but into my heart. It was not my lips you kissed, but my soul.

—**Judy Garland**

The joy that isn't shared dies young.

—**Anne Sexton**

The fountains mingle with the river,
And the rivers with the ocean;
The winds of heaven mix forever,
With a sweet emotion;
Nothing in the world is single;
All things by a law divine

In one another's being mingle;
Why not I with thine?

—**Percy Bysshe Shelley**

The sunlight claps the earth
And the moonbeams kiss the sea:
What are all these kissings worth
If thou kiss not me?

—**Percy Bysshe Shelley**

I arise from dreams of thee
In the first sweet sleep of night,
When the winds are breathing low,
And the stars are shining bright.

—**Percy Bysshe Shelley**

Once he drew with one long kiss
My whole soul through my lips,
As sunlight drinketh dew.

—**Alfred, Lord Tennyson**

Fate, Time, Occasion, Chance, and Change? To these All
things are subject but eternal Love.

—**Percy Bysshe Shelley**

When we are not in love too much, we are not in love
enough.

—**Comte de Bussy-Rabutin**

The best and most beautiful things in the world cannot be
seen or even touched they must be felt with the heart.

—**Helen Keller**

This was love at first sight, love everlasting: a feeling unknown, unhoped for, unexpected—in so far as it could be a matter of conscious awareness; it took entire possession of him, and he understood, with joyous amazement, that this was for life.

—Thomas Mann

As love is a union, it knows no extremes of distance.

—Juana Inés de la Cruz

The love we give away is the only love we keep.

—Elbert Hubbard

When peoples care for you and cry for you, they can straighten out your soul.

—Langston Hughes

Love is the most universal, the most tremendous, and the most mysterious of the cosmic forces.

—Pierre Teilhard de Chardin

No matter what you've done for yourself or for humanity, if you can't look back on having given love and attention to your own family, what have you really accomplished?

—Lee Iacocca

Love has power to give in a moment what toil can scarcely reach in an age.

—Johann Wolfgang von Goethe

The love of God, unutterable and perfect, flows into a pure soul the way light rushes into a transparent object. The more love we receive, the more love we shine forth; so that, as we grow clear and open, the more complete the joy of loving is. And the more souls who resonate together, the greater the intensity of their love for, mirror like, each soul reflects the other.

—**Dante**

Love possesses seven hundred wings, and each one extends from the highest heaven to the lowest earth.

—**Djalal ad-Din Rumi**

By the accident of fortune a man may rule the world for a time, but by virtue of love he may rule the world forever.

—**Lao Tzu**

 Fact

Many of the facts about Lao Tzu, a Chinese philosopher who lived in the sixth century B.C., have been lost to time, but scholars agree he was the author of the *Tao Te Ching* (roughly translated to *The Law and Path of Virtue*) and a seminal force in the early establishment of Taoism.

We don't love qualities, we love persons; sometimes by reason of their defects as well as of their qualities.

—**Jacques Maritain**

Thee lift me, and I'll lift thee, and we'll ascend together.

—**Quaker proverb**

Within you I lose myself
Without you I find myself
Wanting to be lost again.

—**Unknown**

When you love someone, you do not love them all the time,
in exactly the same way, from moment to moment. It is an
impossibility. It is even a lie to pretend to. And yet, this is
exactly what most of us demand. We have so little faith in
the ebb and flow of life, of love, of relationships. We leap
at the flow of time and resist in terror its ebb. We are afraid
it will never return. We insist on permanency, on duration,
on continuity; when the only continuity possible in life, as
in love, is in growth, in fluidity—in freedom. The only real
security is not in owning or possessing, not in demanding
or expecting, not in hoping, even. Security in a relationship
lies neither in looking back to what it was, nor forward to
what it might be, but living in the present and accepting it
as it is now. For relationships, too, must be like islands.
One must accept them for what they are here and now,
within their limits—islands surrounded and interrupted by
the sea, continuously visited and abandoned by the tides.
One must accept the serenity of the winged life, of ebb and
flow, of intermittency.

—**Anne Morrow Lindbergh**

My whole heart for my whole life.

—**French saying**

No one has ever known me as clearly as you. No one has
ever shown me that love allows everything. Not pretty or

safe or easy but something I never knew. Love within reason, that isn't love and I learned that from you.

—Stephen Sondheim

There isn't time—so brief is life—for bickerings, apologies, heartburnings, callings to account. There is only time for loving—and but an instant, so to speak, for that.

—Mark Twain

No cord or cable can draw so forcibly, or bind so fast, as love can do with a single thread.

—Robert Burton

The birthday of my life has come, my love has come to me.

—Christina Rossetti

Shared joy is double joy. Shared sorrow is half sorrow.

—Swedish proverb

Do you want me to tell you something really subversive? Love is everything it's cracked up to be. That's why people are so cynical about it. . . . It really is worth fighting for, being brave for, risking everything for. And the trouble is, if you don't risk anything, you risk even more.

—Erica Jong

He who is in love is wise and is becoming wiser, sees newly every time he looks at the object beloved, drawing from it with his eyes and his mind those virtues which it possesses.

—Ralph Waldo Emerson

My heart to you is given:
Oh, do give yours to me;
We'll lock them up together,
And throw away the key.

—Frederick Saunders

Love won't be tampered with, love won't go away. Push it to one side and it creeps to the other.

—Louise Erdrich

If you live to be a hundred, I want to live to be a hundred minus one day so I never have to live without you.

—A. A. Milne

The first duty of love—is to listen.

—Paul Tillich

He has achieved success who has lived well, laughed often, and loved much.

—Bessie Stanley

It makes no difference how deeply seated may be the trouble, how hopeless the outlook, how muddled the tangle, how great the mistake. A sufficient realization of love will dissolve it all.

—Emmet Fox

I would love to spend all my time writing to you; I'd love to share with you all that goes through my mind, all that weighs on my heart, all that gives air to my soul; phantoms of art, dreams that would be so beautiful if they could come true.

—Luigi Pirandello

The highest happiness on earth is marriage. Every man who is happily married is a successful man even if he has failed in everything else.

—William Lyon Phelps

Let us always meet each other with a smile, for the smile is the beginning of love.

—Mother Teresa

Love feels no burden, thinks nothing of trouble, attempts what is above its strength, pleads no excuse of impossibility; for it thinks all things lawful for itself, and all things possible.

—Thomas à Kempis

In a time when nothing is more certain than change, the commitment of two people to one another has become difficult and rare. Yet, by its scarcity, the beauty and value of this exchange have only been enhanced.

—Robert Sexton

My most brilliant achievement was my ability to be able to persuade my wife to marry me.

—Winston Churchill

As for me, to love you alone, to make you happy, to do nothing which would contradict your wishes, this is my destiny and the meaning of my life.

—Napoleon Bonaparte

Love is the energizing elixir of the universe, the cause and effect of all harmonies.

—Djalal ad-Din Rumi

Love that is hoarded moulds at last
Until we know some day
The only thing we ever have
Is what we give away.

—**Louis Ginsberg**

A loving heart is the truest wisdom.

—**Charles Dickens**

In all the crowded universe
There is but one stupendous word: Love.
There is no tree that rears its crest,
No fern or flower that cleaves the sod
Nor bird that sings above its nest,
But tries to speak this word of God.

—**Josiah Gilbert Holland**

Love is the master key which opens the gates of happiness.

—**Oliver Wendell Holmes**

Love at its highest point—love, sublime, unique, invincible—leads us straight to the brink of the great abyss, for it speaks to us directly of the infinite and of eternity. It is eminently religious.

—**Henri Amiel**

Let us have love and more love; a love that melts all opposition, a love that conquers all foes, a love that sweeps away all barriers, a love that aboundeth in charity, a large-heartedness, tolerance, forgiveness and noble striving, a love that triumphs over all obstacles.

—Abdul Baha

When one has once fully entered the realm of love, the world—no matter how imperfect—becomes rich and beautiful, it consists solely of opportunities for love.

—Søren Kierkegaard

Love, like Death, Levels all ranks, and lays the shepherd's crook Beside the scepter.

—Edward Bulwer-Lytton

Chains do not hold a marriage together. It is threads, hundreds of tiny threads, which sew people together through the years.

—Simone Signoret

Even if marriages are made in heaven, man has to be responsible for the maintenance.

—Unknown

Come live in my heart and pay no rent.

—Samuel Lover

She missed him the days when some pretext served to take him away from her, just as one misses the sun on a cloudy day without having thought much about the sun when it was shining.

—Kate Chopin

There is only one path to Heaven. On Earth, we call it Love.

—**Karen Goldman**

Love can make the summer fly, or a night seem like a lifetime.

—**Andrew Lloyd Webber**

Love demands all, and has a right to all.

—**Ludwig van Beethoven**

Ⓔ *Fact*

Eighteenth-century German composer and pianist Ludwig van Beethoven never married, but he left behind an unsent letter addressed to "Immortal Beloved." Who the lucky lady was has never been verified, but it has been the subject of much debate for almost 200 years. The 1994 film *Immortal Beloved* starring Gary Oldman is a fictional answer to this question.

The most precious possession that ever comes to a man in this world is a woman's heart.

—**Josiah Gilbert Holland**

Not love at first sight, but affection at first glance.

—**Jim Kruta**

We are each of us angels with only one wing. And we can only fly embracing each other.

—**Luciano De Crescenzo**

Married couples who love each other tell each other a thousand things without talking.

—Chinese proverb

If we listened to our intellect, we'd never have a love affair. We'd never have a friendship. . . . Well, that's nonsense. You've got to jump off cliffs all the time and build your wings on the way down.

—Ray Bradbury

A successful marriage requires falling in love many times, always with the same person.

—Mignon McLaughlin

The soul that can speak through the eyes can also kiss with a gaze.

—Gustavo Adolfo Bécquer

Beloved, all that is harsh and difficult I want for myself, and all that is gentle and sweet for thee.

—San Juan de la Cruz

The reduction of the universe to a single being, the expansion of a single being even to God, this is love.

—Victor Hugo

We do not judge the people we love.

—Jean Paul Sartre

A very small degree of hope is sufficient to cause the birth of love.

—Stendhal

There is no remedy for love but to love more.

—Henry David Thoreau

Love is a force more formidable than any other. It is invisible—it cannot be seen or measured, yet it is powerful enough to transform you in a moment, and offer you more joy than any material possession could.

—Barbara De Angelis

I dreamed of a wedding of elaborate elegance; a church filled with flowers and friends. I asked him what kind of wedding he wished for; he said one that would make me his wife.

—Unknown

Love, like virtue, is its own reward.

—John Vanbrugh

Love makes the wildest spirit tame, and the tamest spirit wild.

—Alexis Delp

For what is love itself, for the one we love best? An enfolding of immeasurable cares which yet are better than any joys outside our love.

—George Eliot

The chemist who can extract from his heart's elements, compassion, respect, longing, patience, regret, surprise, and forgiveness and compound them into one can create that atom which is called love.

—Kahlil Gibran

Love is not blind—it sees more, not less. But because it sees more, it is willing to see less.

—Rabbi J. Gordon

It is mind, not body, that makes marriage last.

—Publilius Syrus

Time is too slow for those who wait; too swift for those who fear; too long for those who grieve; too short for those who rejoice. But for those who love, time is eternity.

—Lady Jane Fellowes

Two souls with but a single thought, Two hearts that beat as one.

—Freidrich Halm

Let your love be like the misty rain, coming softly, but flooding the river.

—Madagascan proverb

A successful marriage is not a gift; it is an achievement.

—Ann Landers

Greet each day with your eyes open to beauty, your mind open to change, and your heart open to love.

—Paula Finn

Today I begin to understand what love must be, if it exists. . . . When we are parted, we each feel the lack of the other half of ourselves. We are incomplete like a book in two volumes of which the first has been lost. That is what I imagine love to be: incompleteness in absence.

—Edmond de Goncourt

Love is the ultimate outlaw. It just won't adhere to any rules. The most any of us can do is sign on as its accomplice.

—**Tom Robbins**

Love is, above all, the gift of oneself.

—**Jean Anouilh**

Remember that when you leave this earth, you can take with you nothing that you have received—only what you have given: a full heart enriched by honest service, love, sacrifice and courage.

—**Francis of Assisi**

 Fact

Saint Francis of Assisi was a twelfth-century Italian friar who started the Order of Friars Minor, or the Franciscans. Born into a prosperous family, he lived a worldly, pleasure-filled life as a soldier until he was called to an ascetic life and then a religious life. His followers are noted for their charity to the poor and respect for animals and nature.

Married love between man and woman is bigger than oaths guarded by right of nature.

—**Aeschylus**

When you make the sacrifice in marriage, you're sacrificing not to each other but to unity in a relationship.

—**Joseph Campbell**

Let men tremble to win the hand of a woman, unless they win along with it the utmost passion of her heart.

—Nathaniel Hawthorne

What a grand thing, to be loved! What a grander thing still, to love!

—Victor Hugo

Love is that condition in which the happiness of another person is essential to your own.

—Robert A. Heinlein

All you need in the world is love and laughter. That's all anybody needs. To have love in one hand and laughter in the other.

—August Wilson

All you need for happiness is a good gun, a good horse, and a good wife.

—Daniel Boone

Oh, the comfort, the inexpressible comfort of feeling safe with a person; having neither to weigh thoughts nor measure words, but to pour them all out, chaff and grain together, certain that a faithful hand will take and sift them, keep what is worth keeping, and with a breath of kindness blow the rest away.

—Dinah Maria Mulock Craik

Heaven will be no heaven to me if I do not meet my wife there.

—Andrew Jackson

Love doesn't make the world go 'round. Love is what makes the ride worthwhile.

—Franklin P. Jones

There is no more lovely, friendly and charming relationship, communion or company than a good marriage.

—Martin Luther

Love both gives and receives, and in giving it receives.

—Thomas Merton

Put away the book, the description, the tradition, the authority, and take the journey of self-discovery. Love, and don't be caught in opinions and ideas about what love is or should be. When you love, everything will come right. Love has its own action. Love, and you will know the blessings of it. Keep away from the authority who tells you what love is and what it is not. No authority knows and he who knows cannot tell. Love, and there is understanding.

—Jiddu Krishnamurti

Love is . . . born with the pleasure of looking at each other, it is fed with the necessity of seeing each other, it is concluded with the impossibility of separation.

—José Martí y Pérez

I am, in every thought of my heart, yours.

—Woodrow Wilson

Love is not finding someone to live with; it's finding someone you can't live without.

—Rafael Ortiz

The most wonderful of all things in life, I believe, is the discovery of another human being with whom one's relationship has a glowing depth, beauty, and joy as the years increase. This inner progressiveness of love between two human beings is a most marvelous thing, it cannot be found by looking for it or by passionately wishing for it. It is sort of a Divine accident.

—**Sir Hugh Walpole**

The heart has its reasons that reason does not know.

—**Pascal**

Those who desire to see the living God face to face should not seek Him in the empty firmament of his mind, but in human love.

—**Fyodor Dostoevsky**

We find rest in those we love, and we provide a resting place in ourselves for those who love us.

—**Saint Bernard of Clairvaux**

My love has given you my heart and my soul. They are yours to do with as you please. Please be careful with them.

—**Robert Davis**

May love and laughter light your days, and warm your heart and home. May good and faithful friends be yours wherever you may roam. May peace and plenty bless your world with joy that long endures. May all life's passing seasons bring the best to you and yours.

—**Irish blessing**

May you always have . . .
Walls for the wind
A roof for the rain,
Tea beside the fire
Laughter to cheer you,
Those you love near you
And all your heart might desire!

—**Irish blessing**

What greater thing is there for two human souls than to feel that they are joined together to strengthen each other in all labour, to minister to each other in all sorrow, to share with each other in all gladness, to be one with each other in the silent unspoken memories?

—**George Eliot**

 Fact

George Eliot, born Mary Ann Evans, was a nineteenth-century British author who scandalized society by living openly with her partner George Lewes, who was married to another women with whom he was engaged in an "open marriage" by mutual agreement. They resided happily and productively together for many years until his death.

Love is the only sane and satisfactory answer to the problem of human existence.

—**Erich Fromm**

Since love is the most delicate and total act of a soul, it will reflect the state and nature of the soul. If the individual is not sensitive, how can his love be sentient? If he is not profound, how can his love be deep? As one is, so is his love.

—José Ortega y Gasset

The truth is that there is only one terminal dignity—love. And the story of a love is not important—what is important is that one is capable of love. It is perhaps the only glimpse we are permitted of eternity.

—Helen Hayes

Love keeps the cold out better than a cloak.

—Henry Wadsworth Longfellow

You will reciprocally promise love, loyalty, and matrimonial honesty. We only want for you this day that these words constitute the principle of your entire life; that with the help of divine grace you will observe these solemn vows that today, before God, you formulate.

—Pope John Paul II

Chapter 7
Inspirational Words

There's a chance someone has already found the words to express exactly how you feel about your beloved. You can borrow the words of literature's greats for inspiration or for your vows themselves. You can use a quotation or passage as your entire wedding vow or use a short quote to get you started and expand upon the theme in your own words.

Great Names in Romantic Writing

Anyone can whip out a pretty line or two about their innermost feelings. It takes a special talent to do so over and over again without getting bogged down in treacly bilge. Here are some of the world's greatest love poets.

. . . Love is not love
Which alters when it alteration finds,
Or bends with the remover to remove:
O, no! it is an ever-fixed mark,
That looks on tempests and is never shaken;
It is the star to every wandering bark,
Whose worth's unknown, although his height be taken.

—**William Shakespeare**

Love's mysteries in souls do grow,
But yet the body is his book.

—**John Donne**

Love, all alike, no season knows, nor clime,
Nor hours, days, months, which are the rags of time.

—**John Donne**

My bounty is as boundless as the sea.
My love as deep; the more I give to thee,
The more I have, for both are infinite.

—**William Shakespeare**

I wonder, by my troth, what thou and I did till we lov'd?

—**John Donne**

Two human loves make one divine.

—**Elizabeth Barrett Browning**

Love comforteth like sunshine after rain.

—William Shakespeare

Love sought is good, but given unsought is better.

—William Shakespeare

So dear I love him that with him,
All deaths I could endure.
Without him, live no life.

—William Shakespeare

The face of all the world is changed, I think,
Since first I heard the footsteps of thy soul.

—Elizabeth Barrett Browning

Love me, sweet, with all thou art,
Feeling, thinking, seeing,—
Love me in the lightest part,
Love me in full being.

—Elizabeth Barrett Browning

Whoever lives true life will love true love.

—Elizabeth Barrett Browning

If music be the food of love, play on.

—William Shakespeare

The one thing we can never get enough of is love. And the one thing we never give enough is love.

—Henry Miller

Every man has his own destiny: the only imperative is to follow it, to accept it, no matter where it leads him.

—Henry Miller

I love thee, I love but thee
With a love that shall not die
Till the sun grows cold
And the stars grow old.

—**William Shakespeare**

What's earth with all its art, verse, music, worth compared
with love, found, gained and kept?

—**Robert Browning**

Long after moments of closeness have passed,
A part of you remains with me
And warms the places your hands have touched
And hastens my heart for your return.
Such is my love, to thee I so belong,
That for thy right myself will bear all wrong.

—**William Shakespeare**

Grow old along with me! The best is yet to be. The last of
life, for which the first was made. Our times are in his hand
Who saith, A whole I planned; Youth shows but half. Trust
God; see all, nor be afraid!

—**Robert Browning**

How do I love thee? Let me count the ways.
I love thee to the depth and breadth and height
My soul can reach, when feeling out of sight
For the ends of Being and ideal Grace.
I love thee to the level of every day's
Most quiet need, by sun and candle-light.
I love thee freely, as men strive for Right;
I love thee purely, as they turn from Praise.

I love thee with the passion put to use
In my old griefs, and with my childhood's faith.
I love thee with a love I seemed to lose
With my lost saints—I love thee with the breath,
Smiles, tears of all my life!—and if God choose,
I shall but love thee better after death.

—Elizabeth Barrett Browning

Fact

Elizabeth Barrett Browning had to elope in order to escape her tyrannical father's demand that she (or any of her eleven siblings) never marry. She and fellow poet Robert Browning fled England together and lived happily in Italy with their son "Pen" until her death in 1861.

If thou must love me, let it be for nought
Except for love's sake only. Do not say,
I love her for her smile . . . her look . . . her way
Of speaking gently—for a trick of thought
That falls in well with mine, and, certes, brought
A sense of pleasant ease on such a day—
For these things in themselves, Beloved, may
Be changed, or change for thee—and love so wrought,
May be unwrought so. Neither love me for
Thine own dear pity's wiping my cheeks dry,—
A creature might forget to weep, who bore
Thy comfort long, and lose thy love thereby!

But love me for love's sake, that evermore
Thou mayst love on, through love's eternity.

—Elizabeth Barrett Browning

She walks in beauty, like the night
Of cloudless climes and starry skies;
And all that's best of dark and bright
Meet in her aspect and her eyes:
This mellowed to that tender light
Which heaven to gaudy day denies.
One shade the more, one ray the less,
Had half impaired the nameless grace
Which waves in every raven tress,
Or softly lightens o'er her face;
Where thoughts serenely sweet express
How pure, how dear their dwelling place.

—Lord Byron

So, fall asleep love, loved by me. . . .For I know love, I am
loved by thee.

—Robert Browning

Mine ear is much enamoured to thy note;
So is mine eye enthralled to thy shape,
And thy fair virtue's force perforce doth move me
On the first view to say, to swear, I love thee.

—William Shakespeare

Did my heart love till now? Forswear it sight, for I never
saw true beauty till tonight.

—William Shakespeare

So dear I love him that with him, all deaths I could endure.
Without him, live no life.

—William Shakespeare

'Tis sweet to know there is an eye will mark
Our coming, and look brighter when we come.

—Lord Byron

My face in thine eye, thine in mine appears,
And true plain hearts do in the faces rest;
Where can we find two better hemispheres,
Without sharp north, without declining west?
Whatever dies, was not mix'd equally;
If our two loves be one, or, thou and I
Love so alike, that none do slacken, none can die.

—John Donne

I'll be as patient as a gentle stream
And make a pastime of each weary step,
Till the last step have brought me to my love;
And there I'll rest, as after much turmoil
A blessed soul doth in Elysium.

—William Shakespeare

My heart is ever at your service.

—William Shakespeare

They do not love that do not show their love.

—William Shakespeare

Love will find a way through paths where wolves fear to prey.

—Lord Byron

Doubt thou the stars are fire;
Doubt that the sun doth move:
Doubt truth to be a liar;
But never doubt, I love.

—**William Shakespeare**

Earth holds no other like to thee,
Or if it doth, in vain for me.

—**Lord Byron**

No man is an island, entire of himself; every man is a piece of the continent.

—**John Donne**

An Ode to Friendship

It used to be that marriage and friendship were two separate and distinct entities. Marriage was a partnership, and friends provided all the fun and camaraderie. As you and your fiancé probably know, friendship is the glue that will keep your marriage together just as it's kept your romance alive. Maybe you began as friends and grew into a couple or you started dating and forged a friendship in the process. Either way, you might want to include a quote or a reading that will address the future of your beautiful friendship.

A friend might well be reckoned the masterpiece of nature.

—**Ralph Waldo Emerson**

Everybody needs one essential friend.

—**William Glasser**

What is a friend? One soul in two bodies.

—Aristotle

There's lots of things
With which I'm blessed,
Tho' my life's been both Sunny and Blue,
But of all my blessings,
This one's the best:
To have a friend like you.
In times of trouble
Friends will say,
"Just ask . . . I'll help you through it."
But you don't wait for me to ask,
You just get up and you do it!
And I can think
Of nothing in life
That I could more wisely do,
Than know a friend,
And be a friend,
And love a friend . . . like you.

—Unknown

Two may talk together under the same roof for many years, yet never really meet; and two others at first speech are old friends.

—Mary Catherwood

A single rose can be my garden . . . a single friend, my world.

—Leo Buscaglia

Plant a seed of friendship; reap a bouquet of happiness.

—**Lois L. Kaufman**

It takes a long time to grow an old friend.

—**John Leonard**

One of the most beautiful qualities of true friendship is to understand and to be understood.

—**Seneca**

Friends are not necessary to live. They do, however, make life worth living.

—**C. S. Lewis**

All love that has not friendship for its base is like a mansion built upon the sand.

—**Ella Wheeler Wilcox**

Fact

Ella Wheeler Wilcox was a nineteenth-century poet from Wisconsin, known for many of her early temperance poems. She came from a family of amateur poets and said she wrote poetry because she felt compelled to. Wilcox reportedly said that her religion was "the art of being kind."

Remember, the greatest gift is not found in a store nor under a tree, but in the hearts of true friends.

—**Cindy Lew**

A true friend unbosoms freely, advises justly, assists readily, adventures boldly, takes all patiently, defends courageously, and continues a friend unchangeably.

—William Penn

Friends will not only live in harmony, but in melody.

—Henry David Thoreau

Our most intimate friend is not he to whom we show the worst, but the best, of our nature.

—Nathaniel Hawthorne

To bear each other's burdens, never to ask each other for anything inconsistent with virtue and rectitude, and not only to serve and love but also to respect each other.

—Cicero

Let us be grateful to people who make us happy; they are the charming gardeners who make our souls blossom.

—Marcel Proust

Friendship is a strong and habitual inclination in two persons to promote the good and happiness of one another.

—Eustace Budgell

Friendship improves happiness and abates misery, by the doubling of our joy and the dividing of our grief.

—Cicero

The soul needs friendship, the heart needs love.

—Ed Habib

We are all travelers in the wilderness of this world, and the best that we can find in our travels is an honest friend.

—Robert Louis Stevenson

Friends . . .
They cherish one another's hopes.
They are kind to one another's dreams.

—Henry David Thoreau

A friend is one who knows you and loves you just the same.

—Elbert Hubbard

The glory of friendship is not the outstretched hand,
nor the kindly smile nor the joy of companionship;
it is the spiritual inspiration that comes to one when he discovers that someone else believes in him and is willing to trust him.

—Ralph Waldo Emerson

A friend hears the song of my heart and sings it to me when my memory fails.

—Unknown

A blessed thing it is for any man or woman to have a friend, one human soul whom we can trust utterly, who knows the best and worst of us, and who loves us in spite of all our faults.

—Charles Kingsley

What do we live for,
if not to make life less difficult
for each other?

—George Eliot

In everyone's life, at some time, our inner fire goes out.
It is then burst into flame by an encounter with another
human being.
We should all be thankful for those people who rekindle the
inner spirit.

—Albert Schweitzer

Once I knew only darkness and stillness . . .
my life was without past or future . . .
but a little word from the fingers of another
fell into my hand that clutched at emptiness,
and my heart leaped to the rapture of living.

—Helen Keller

True friendship is a plant of slow growth,
and must undergo and withstand the shocks of adversity,
before it is entitled to the appellation.

—George Washington

Be slow to fall into friendship; but when thou art in, continue firm and constant.

—Socrates

To know someone, here or there, with whom you feel there is understanding in spite of distances or thoughts unexpressed—that can make of this earth a garden.

—Johann Wolfgang von Goethe

Love is friendship that has caught fire.

—**Ann Landers**

Who much to be prized and esteemed is a friend,
On whom we may always with safety depend;
Our joys when extended will always increase,
And griefs when divided are hushed into peace.

—**Aesop**

Best friend, my wellspring in the wilderness!

—**George Eliot**

Blessed is the influence of one true, loving human soul on another.

—**George Eliot**

Each friend represents a world in us, a world possibly not born until they arrive, and it is only by this meeting that a new world is born.

—**Anaïs Nin**

A friend is one that knows you as you are, understands where you have been, accepts what you have become, and still, gently allows you to grow.

—**William Shakespeare**

Treasure each other in the recognition that we do not know how long we shall have each other.

—**Joshua Loth Liebman**

Don't walk in front of me, I may not follow.
Don't walk behind me, I may not lead.

Just walk beside me and be my friend.

—**Albert Camus**

The greatest sweetener of human life is Friendship. To raise this to the highest pitch of enjoyment, is a secret which but few discover.

—**Joseph Addison**

A friend is someone you want to be around when you feel like being by yourself.

—**Barbara Burrow**

Sometimes, when one person is missing, the whole world seems depopulated.

—**Alphonse de Lamartine**

True friends don't spend time gazing into each others' eyes. They may show great tenderness towards each other, but they face in the same direction—toward common projects, goals—above all, towards a common Lord.

—**C. S. Lewis**

Hold a true friend with both hands.

—**Nigerian proverb**

My best friend is the one who brings out the best in me.

—**Henry Ford**

Friendship's the wine of life.

—**Edward Young**

A friend is, as it were, a second self.

—**Cicero**

Grief can take care of itself, but to get the full value out of joy, you must have someone to divide it with.

—**Mark Twain**

I could do without many things with no hardship—you are not one of them.

—**Ashleigh Brilliant**

Continue to be my friend, as you will always find me yours.

—**Ludwig van Beethoven**

Chapter 8
Great Love Lines
from the Movies

L et's face it, some of the best love lines come from the movies. Who doesn't get a shiver up their spine when they hear Rhett Butler growl, "Frankly Scarlet, I don't give a damn!" knowing full well that he does? If you're still stuck for inspiration, here are some time-tested, hanky-wringing lines from some favorite films that will be a hit with your betrothed and guests.

I hate the way you talk to me and the way you cut your hair. I hate the way you drive my car; I hate it when you stare. I hate your big dumb combat boots and the way you read my mind. I hate you so much that it makes me sick. It even makes me rhyme. I hate the way you're always right. I hate it when you lie. I hate it when you make me laugh, even worse when you make me cry. I hate the way you're not around, and the fact that you didn't call. But mostly I hate the way I don't hate you. Not even close, not even a little bit, not even at all.

—10 Things I Hate About You

 Fact

10 Things I Hate About You is an updating of William Shakespeare's The Taming of The Shrew. When you are stealing, steal from the best. For vow writers it pays to, as the song goes, "Brush Up Your Shakespeare" (which, by the way, is from Kiss Me Kate, another updating of The Taming of the Shrew).

You were to me something apart from common life . . . a thing noble, pure. The world seemed to me finer because you were in it, goodness more real because you lived.

—An Ideal Husband

I might be the only one who appreciates how amazing you are in every single thing that you do, and . . . how you say what you mean, and how you almost always mean something that's all about being straight and good. I think most people miss that about you, and I watch them, wondering how they can watch you bring their food and clear their tables and never get that they just met the greatest woman alive. And the fact that I get it makes me feel good, about me.

—As Good As It Gets

This kind of certainty comes but once in a lifetime.
—The Bridges of Madison County

You make me want to be a better man.
—As Good As It Gets

 Fact

Jack Nicholson and Helen Hunt both won Oscars for *As Good As It Gets*, but each of their characters were deeply flawed. This makes them great characters for actors to portray, but not the best romantic role models.

It seems right now that all I've ever done in my life is making my way here to you.
—The Bridges of Madison County

I'd ask you about love, you'd probably quote me a sonnet. But you've never looked at a woman and been totally vulnerable. Known someone that could level you with her eyes, feeling like God put an angel on earth just for you, who could rescue you from the depths of hell. And you wouldn't know what it's like to be her angel, to have that love for her, be there forever, through anything.

— *Good Will Hunting*

Ⓔ Fact

Matt Damon and Ben Affleck won an Oscar for best original screenplay for *Good Will Hunting*. At the time, neither had ever wed, although now both are happily married with kids.

A beautiful girl can make you dizzy. . . . She can make you feel high, full of the single greatest commodity known to man—promise. Promise of a better day. Promise of a greater hope. Promise of a new tomorrow. This particular aura can be found in the gait of a beautiful girl. In her smile, in her soul, the way she makes every rotten little thing about life seem like it's going to be okay.

— *Beautiful Girls*

If there's any kind of magic in this world, it must be in the attempt of understanding someone, sharing something. I know, it's almost impossible to succeed, but . . . who cares, really? The answer must be in the attempt.

— *Before Sunrise*

I will love you my whole life. You and no other.

— *Braveheart*

At last my heart's an open door
And my secret love's no secret anymore.

—Calamity Jane

When you love someone, you've gotta trust them. There's no other way. You've got to give them the key to everything that's yours. Otherwise, what's the point?

—Casino

Essential

The sentiment expressed by the *Casino* character played by Robert De Niro leads to big problems for him. In terms of using it in a vow, you may not want your audience to associate your love with organized crime. In this case, you may want to echo the sentiment without attributing the source.

I love you. Very simple, very truly. You're the epitome of every attribute and quality I've ever looked for in another person. . . . I can't stand next to you without wanting to hold you. I can't look into your eyes without feeling that longing you only read about in trashy romance novels. I can't talk to you without wanting to express my love for everything you are. . . . I've never felt this before, and I like who I am because of it. . . . There isn't another soul on this . . . planet who's ever made me half the person I am when I'm with you. . . . I'm forever changed because of who you are and what you've meant to me.

—Chasing Amy

I would rather have had one breath of her hair, one kiss from her mouth, one touch of her hand, than eternity without it.

—*City of Angels*

I want the last face you see in this world to be the face of love. . . . I'll be the face of love for you.

—*Dead Man Walking*

I need to feel strongly, to love and to admire, just as desperately as I need to breathe.

—*The Diving Bell and the Butterfly*

Anything less than mad, passionate, extraordinary love is a waste of your time. There are too many mediocre things in life to deal with and love shouldn't have to be one of them.

—*Dream for an Insomniac*

A life without love is no life at all.

—*Ever After*

I take the good with the bad. I can't love people in pieces.

—*First Knight*

I only know one way to love my lord, and that is body and heart and soul.

—*First Knight*

I love you with every cell, with every atom. I love you on a subatomic level.

—*Flubber*

Love is a gift . . . not an obligation.

—*Fools Rush In*

Whenever I despair, I remember that the way of truth and love has always won. There may be tyrants and murderers, and for a time, they may seem invincible, but in the end, they always fail. Think of it: always.

—Gandhi

There are only four questions of value in life. . . . What is sacred? Of what is the spirit made? What is worth living for, and what is worth dying for? The answer to each is the same: only love.

—Don Juan DeMarco

Ⓔ *Alert!*

The great romantic poet Lord Byron (1788–1824) is listed as cowriter on the *Don Juan DeMarco* screenplay—quite impressive for a man who had been dead for 175 years before the movie was made. One of the great Romantic poets, Byron had a way with words. You might check out some of his writing for inspiration when you write your vows.

So how does it happen, great love? Nobody knows . . . but what I can tell you is that it happens in the blink of an eye. One moment you're enjoying your life, and the next you're wondering how you ever lived without them.

—Hitch

Young lovers seek perfection. Old lovers learn the art of sewing shreds together and of seeing beauty in a multiplicity of patches.

—How to Make an American Quilt

I am not full of virtues and noble qualities. I love. That is all. But I love strongly, exclusively and steadfastly.

—Impromptu

What is it you want, Mary? What do you want? You want the moon? Just say the word and I'll throw a lasso around it and pull it down.

—It's a Wonderful Life

Essential

The American Film Institute named *It's a Wonderful Life* the most powerful movie, the most inspirational movie, and the twentieth greatest movie of all time. Bring the vow home by relating how the movie shows the impact one person has on the lives of others, how the movie shows a couple at their best, or how the couple found answers for each other.

I love you. You complete me.

—Jerry Maguire

You had me at 'Hello.'

—Jerry Maguire

Love is eternal. It has been the strongest motivation for human actions throughout history. Love is stronger than life. It reaches beyond the dark shadow of death.

—***Laura***

I would rather share one lifetime with you than face all the ages of this world alone.

—***The Lord of the Rings: The Fellowship of the Ring***

Love is passion, obsession, something you can't live without. Fall head over heels, find someone who you can love like crazy that will love you the same way back. How do you find them? Well, forget your head and listen to your heart . . . the truth is, there is no sense living your life without this.

—***Meet Joe Black***

Every step I took since the moment I could walk was a step towards finding you.

—***Message in a Bottle***

I love you. Not like they told you love is—and I didn't know this either, but love don't make things nice—it ruins everything. It breaks your heart. It makes things a mess. We aren't here to make things perfect. The snowflakes are perfect. The stars are perfect. Not us.

—***Moonstruck***

The greatest thing you'll ever learn is just to love and be loved in return.

—***Moulin Rouge***

Never knew I could feel like this. Like I've never seen the sky before. Want to vanish inside your kiss, every day I'm loving you more and more. Listen to my heart, can you hear it sing? Come back to me—and forgive everything. Seasons change, winter to spring. I love you. Until the end of time.

—***Moulin Rouge***

With the woman that you love at your side to stand behind you, a man can move mountains with his bare heart.

—***Movie Movie***

When you kiss someone, everything around you becomes hazy and the only thing you focus on is that one person. And you realize that that person is the only person you're supposed to be kissing for the rest of your life and for one moment you get this amazing gift and you want to laugh and you want to cry cause you feel so lucky that you've found it and so scared that it'll go away, all at the same time.

—***Never Been Kissed***

That's my sweetheart in there. Wherever she is, that's where my home is.

—***The Notebook***

So it's not gonna be easy. It's gonna be really hard. We're gonna have to work at this every day, but I want to do that because I want you. I want all of you, forever, you and me, every day.

—***The Notebook***

The best love is the kind that weakens the soul, that makes us reach for more, that plants fire in our hearts and brings peace to our minds. And that's what you've given me. That's what I hope to give to you forever.

—The Notebook

Ⓔ Essential

The Notebook tells two love stories—those of the younger couple and the older couple, two visions of the same love. Let that passion of youth and lifelong love resonate with you. Let the vows you are writing show the whole spectrum of love over your lifetime together.

Poets often describe love as an emotion that we can't control, one that overwhelms logic and common sense. That's what it's like for me. I didn't plan on falling in love with you, and I doubt that you planned on falling in love with me. But once we met, it was clear that neither of us could control what was happening to us. We fell in love, despite our differences, and once we did, something rare and beautiful was created. For me, love like that has happened only once, and that's why every minute we spent together has been seared in my memory. I'll never forget a single moment of it.

—The Notebook

In my heart I know you intimately.

> *—Persuasion*

You pierce my soul!

> *—Persuasion*

You have bewitched me, body and soul, and I love and love and love you. And I never wish to be parted from you from this day on.

> *—Pride and Prejudice*

True love. You know, when you're old and you're wrinkly and you're sitting there gumming your food and your husband looks at you and even though he doesn't see you very well anymore, he can see in your eyes the whole world: the future, the past, everything that was good and even things that were bad, and he can still say, 'There is my queen, and what a privilege it has been to love her.'

> *—Prince Charming*

That day, she was amazed to discover that when he was saying, "As you wish," what he really meant was, "I love you." And even more amazing was the day she realized she truly loved him back.

> *—The Princess Bride*

Westley and I are joined by the bonds of love. And you cannot track that, not with a thousand bloodhounds, and you cannot break it, not with a thousand swords.

> *—The Princess Bride*

I guarantee there'll be tough times. I guarantee that at some time, one or both of us is gonna want to get out of this thing. But I also guarantee that if I don't ask you to be mine, I'll regret it for the rest of my life, because I know, in my heart, you're the only one for me.

—Runaway Bride

Yours has been the most important friendship of my life.

—Sense and Sensibility

Essential

True love may not have triumphed for the caddish Mr. Willoughby, played by Greg Wise in the 1995 interpretation of Jane Austen's classic *Sense and Sensibility*, but it did in real life. Behind the scenes, Wise won the heart of the film's star and screen-writer, Emma Thompson. Today the pair are married and the parents of a daughter.

It was a million tiny little things that, when you added them all up, they meant we were suppose to be together . . . and I knew it. I knew it the very first time I touched her. It was like coming home . . . only to no home I'd ever known . . . I was just taking her hand to help her out of a car and I knew. It was like . . . magic.

—Sleepless in Seattle

The man of my dreams has almost faded now. The one I have created in my mind. The sort of man each woman dreams of in the deepest and most secret reaches of her heart. I can almost see him now before me. What would I say to him, if he were really here? Forgive me, I have never known this feeling. I've lived without it all my life. Is it any wonder, then, that I fail to recognize you? You, who brought it to me for the first time. Is there any way I can tell you how my life has changed? Any way at all to let you know what sweetness you have given me? There is so much to say . . . I cannot find the words. Except for these—I love you! Such would I say to him, if he were really here.

> **—Somewhere in Time**

None of those other things make a difference. Love is the strongest thing in the world, you know. Nothing can touch it. Nothing comes close. If we love each other, we're safe from it all. Love is the biggest thing there is.

> **—Snow Falling on Cedars**

I know there'll be risks, but I want to face them with you. It's wrong that we should be only half alive . . . half of ourselves.

> **—Spider-Man 2**

I've always been big on happy endings. You see, to me, the most romantic, beautiful love stories ever were the ones where two people meet, fall in love, and then fifty, sixty years later one of them dies and then a few days after that the other one dies because they just can't bear to live without each other.

> **—The Story of Us**

You know you don't have to act with me, Steve. You don't have to say anything, and you don't have to do anything.

Not a thing. Oh, maybe just whistle. You know how to whistle, don't you, Steve? You just put your lips together and . . . blow.

—To Have and Have Not

Ⓔ *Essential*

Director Howard Hawks offered the luminous Lauren Bacall the opportunity to star with either Cary Grant or Humphrey Bogart in her feature film debut. She chose Bogart. They fell madly in love during the film shoot and were married for twelve years until his death in 1957. In honor of the famous line above, Bacall allegedly requested that her husband be buried with a small gold whistle.

We come to love not by finding a perfect person, but by learning to see an imperfect person perfectly.

—To Love and Be Loved

The world is moved by love. We kneel before it in awe.

—The Village

What good is it to tell you you are in my every thought from the time I wake? What good can come from my saying that I sometimes cannot think clearly or do my work properly? What gain can rise of my telling you the only time I feel fear as others do is when I think of you in harm? I fear for your safety before all others.

—The Village

If you find somebody you can love, you can't let that get away.

—The Wedding Singer

I wanna make you smile whenever you're sad
Carry you around when your arthritis is bad.
I wanna grow old with you
So let me do the dishes in the kitchen sink
Put you to bed when you've had too much to drink.
Oh I could be the man to grow old with you.
I wanna grow old with you.

—The Wedding Singer

She has 600 different smiles. They can light up your life. They can make you laugh out loud, just like that. They can even make you cry, just like that. That's just with her smiles.

—When a Man Loves a Woman

Ⓔ Essential

Director Rob Reiner came up with the idea for his 1989 blockbuster *When Harry Met Sally* partly in reaction to his post-divorce depression. Ironically, he met his new wife, Michele, while working on the movie. She came to the set one day to visit her friend Barry Sonnenfeld, the director of photography.

I love that you get cold when it's seventy-one degrees out. I love that it takes you an hour and a half to order a sandwich. I love that you get a little crinkle in your nose when you're looking at me like I'm nuts. I love that after I spend the day with you, I can still smell your perfume on my clothes. And I love that you are the last person I want to talk to before I go to sleep at night. And it's not because I'm lonely, and it's not because it's New Year's Eve. I came here tonight because when you realize you want to spend the rest of your life with somebody, you want the rest of your life to start as soon as possible.

—When Harry Met Sally

Chapter 9
At One with Nature

It is easy to get swept away by the beauty that is the great outdoors and wish to incorporate it into your ceremony. Both romance and nature are themes that have inspired poets for centuries, triggering some of the most stirring works in the English-speaking world. Spring, summer, and fall are especially popular times for al fresco ceremonies, and a nod to Mother Nature is not out of place.

Vows for Equinoxes and Solstices

Exchanging vows on the day the seasons change is a unique way of underscoring your wedding's significance as a new beginning. You can draw attention to this by mentioning it in your vows.

Vernal Equinox

If you or your partner is seasonally attuned, you may want to personalize your wedding by incorporating some kind of seasonal imagery in your words, such as these spring vows.

Vow 1

- With spring comes rebirth, and with this ceremony we celebrate our new life together. _____, I take you as my husband/wife and vow to honor always the ever-renewing force of life that is the source of our love.

Vow 2

- **Bride**: Initially, March was the first month of the year because it was the first month in which signs of new growth were visible after the ravages of winter.
- **Groom**: Today we begin our own new spring together.
- **Bride**: From this day forward, _____, March ____ will mark our new beginning—the first day of our life together as a married couple. On this day, and before these witnesses, I give myself to you as your wife.

🥢 **Groom**: From this day forward, _____, March ____ will mark our new beginning—the first day of our life together as a married couple. On this day, and before these witnesses, I give myself to you as your husband.

Ⓔ *Essential*

If you're getting married near a beach, volcano, vineyard, or other outdoor site, a reading that acknowledges or incorporates those elements would be very welcome. Your guests will appreciate the creative touch, and it will make your ceremony stand out in a sea of weddings.

Summer Solstice

Whether you plan to walk along the beach or bask in the air-conditioning of a Victorian villa as you take your vows, summer is a great time to take the plunge. The weather is warm, the trees are in full leaf, and the kids are out of school and ready to play.

Vow 1

🥢 **Bride**: Some say June was named to honor Juno, the goddess of marriage and fertility.

🥢 **Groom**: In her honor, the Romans held a festival on the first day of this enchanting month.

🌺 **Bride**: On this June day, before this honored assembly, _____, I give myself to you as your wife. May our days be many and joyous.

🌺 **Groom**: On this June day, before this honored assembly, _____, I give myself to you as your husband. May our days be many and joyous.

Vow 2

🌺 Now, with summer full in its glory, we join hands and take up our new roles as husband and wife._____, I promise to love and be true to you from this day forward. May our love be as warm and as enduring as the sweetest day of summer.

Vow 3

🌺 **Groom**: _____, today I offer myself to you as your husband, forsaking all others, and sure of the power of a love as rare as gold and as rich as the fullest day of summer. I will stand by your side forever.

🌺 **Bride**: _____, today I offer myself to you as your wife, forsaking all others, and sure of the power of a love as rare as gold and as rich as the fullest day of summer. I will stand by your side forever.

Autumnal Equinox

The autumnal equinox conjures images of fall foliage and apple picking. It is a very picturesque time to get married.

Vow 1

❦ Today, on the ____ day of the harvest month of September, we reap the bounty of our love, beginning our life together as husband and wife. _____, I give myself to you as your partner from this day forward, with thanks and with joy as we prepare to share in all the days of love to come.

Vow 2

❦ The leaves change and the seasons turn, but our love is constant. _____, I join my life with yours on this day and for all the days to come. You are the one with whom I choose to spend all the seasons of my life.

Winter Solstice

It's the shortest day of the year, but dazzling white snow and icicles can make your wedding day very romantic.

❦ _____, we commit ourselves to each other in a time of winter, but the love that brings us here today is the warmest thing I have ever known in my life. I give myself to you as your husband/wife from this day forward.

Nature Love Poems

There are countless poems that pay homage to the great outdoors. The Romantic period, which extended roughly from 1820 to the end of the nineteenth century, was particularly known for its romantic look at love and the outside world.

William Blake

William Blake's (1757–1827) only formal education was in art. Trained as an engraver, he married an illiterate grocer's daughter and, much like the rhyme "Peter, Peter Pumpkin Eater," he "taught her how to read and spell." Whether "he loved her very well" is up for debate. Rumor says he did, but many of his later poems rail against female jealousy and possessiveness, suggesting that all was not quiet on the domestic front. Nonetheless, he left a large repository of poetry regaling the wonders of nature, like these first two stanzas from "Song."

Song

How sweet I roam'd from field to field,
    And tasted all the summer's pride,
Till I the prince of love beheld,
    Who in the sunny beams did glide!
He shew'd me lilies for my hair,
    And blushing roses for my brow;
He led me through his gardens fair,
    Where all his golden pleasures grow.

Robert Burns

Scotsman Robert Burns (1757–96) is best known for his poem "Auld Lang Syne," but he wrote many others over the course of his short but colorful life. When he was not scribbling, he scandalized Edinburgh society by openly enjoying the company of many women and siring numerous illegitimate children before finally marrying his mistress Jean Armour. His appreciation for the fairer sex is aptly represented in "A Red, Red Rose," which, like many of his most popular works, is written in the Scots dialect.

A Red, Red Rose

O My Luve's like a red, red rose,
    That's newly sprung in June;
O My Luve's like the melodie
    That's sweetly played in tune.
As fair art thou, my bonnie lass,
    So deep in Luve am I;
And I will luve thee still, my dear,
    Till a' the seas gang dry.
Till a' the seas gang dry, my dear,
    And the rocks melt wi' the sun:
O I will love thee still, my dear,
    While the sands o' life shall run.
And fare thee weel, my only luve,
    And fare thee weel ahile!
And I will come again, my luve,
    Though it were ten thousand mile.

Lord Byron

Even by the dissolute standards of Regency England, George Gordon, Lord Byron (1788–1824), lived life in the fast lane. Openly admired and pursued by legions of women (and reportedly men) for his remarkable beauty, Byron's many passions included an intense childhood fixation for a female cousin, a complicated affair with the tantrum-prone Lady Caroline Lamb, an incestuous relationship with a half-sister, Augusta Leigh, and a liaison with Percy Shelley's teenaged sister-in-law, Claire Clairmont, with whom he had a child. It was the fallout from the affair with Augusta that finally drove him from England. Comfortably ensconced in the warmer and more liberal climate of Italy, Byron finally settled down to relative domestic stability with a young Italian countess. He was inspired to write "She Walks in Beauty" the day after he met a beautiful young relative by marriage who was wearing a black mourning dress with beads.

She Walks in Beauty

She walks in beauty, like the night
    Of cloudless climes and starry skies;
And all that's best of dark and bright
    Meet in her aspect and her eyes:
Thus mellowed to that tender light
    Which heaven to gaudy day denies.
One shade the more, one ray the less,
    Had half impaired the nameless grace
Which waves in every raven tress,
    Or softly lightens o'er her face;
Where thoughts serenely sweet express
    How pure, how dear their dwelling place.
And on that cheek, and o'er that brow,

So soft, so calm, yet eloquent,
The smiles that win, the tints that glow,
But tell of days in goodness spent,
A mind at peace with all below,
A heart whose love is innocent!

Samuel Taylor Coleridge

Samuel Taylor Coleridge (1772–1834) was remarkably productive in spite of many physical ailments, the opium he took to dull them, an unhappy marriage he felt forced into, a hopeless passion for an unavailable woman, and a falling out with his dearest friend and fellow poet William Wordsworth. He eventually made peace with his demons, but it is interesting to note that many of his most productive years were also his darkest. These first two stanzas from "Recollections of Love" date from that period.

Recollections of Love

How warm this woodland wild recess!
Love surely hath been breathing here;
And this sweet bed of heath, my dear!
Swells up, then sinks with faint caress,
As if to have you yet more near.
Eight springs have flown since last I lay
On seaward Quantock's heathy hills,
Where quiet sounds from hidden rills
Float here and there, like things astray,
And high o'erhead the sky-lark shrills.

Emily Dickinson

Emily Dickinson (1830–86) was born into a prominent Puritan family in Amherst, Massachusetts. Highly
educated for a nineteenth-century woman, she was born
and died in the same house and passed many happy
hours alone in her austere room, working on her poetry.
She eschewed the more florid style of many of her con-
temporaries in favor of more economical, frank, and witty
works.

Wild Nights! Wild Nights!
Wild Nights! Wild Nights!
Were I with thee,
Wild Nights should be
Our luxury!
Futile the winds
To a heart in port—
Done with the compass,
Done with the chart!
Rowing in Eden!
Ah! the sea!
Might I but moor
To-night in Thee!

Nathaniel Hawthorne

Best known as the author of *The Scarlet Letter*,
Nathaniel Hawthorne (1804–64) is believed to have written that book out of the guilt he felt as a descendant of
one of the judges who presided over the infamous Salem

witch trials in the late seventeenth century. He spent much of his childhood in solitude in the great outdoors and with his books, including works by Shakespeare and *The Pilgrim's Progress*, and was heavily influenced by both. Admired by many of his peers for delving into a deeper level of insight than was fashionable at the time, he is still read and lauded by many today.

Address to the Moon

How sweet the silver Moon's pale ray,
Falls trembling on the distant bay,
O'er which the breezes sigh no more,
Nor billows lash the sounding shore.
Say, do the eyes of those I love,
Behold thee as thou soar'st above,
Lonely, majestic and serene,
The calm and placid evening's Queen?
Say, if upon thy peaceful breast,
Departed spirits find their rest,
For who would wish a fairer home,
Than in that bright, refulgent dome?

John Keats

John Keats (1795–1821) was short, poor, orphaned, and left in the care of indifferent overseers. He was madly in love with a woman he could not marry and haunted by a premonition that he would die early. Had he lived longer, many believe he would have developed into one of the greatest English-speaking poets of all time. As it is, we must be satisfied with what he did accomplish, including these romantic lines from *Endymion: A Poetic Romance.*

Endymion: A Poetic Romance

A thing of beauty is a joy forever;
Its loveliness increases; it will never
Pass into nothingness; but still we keep
A bower quiet for us, and a sleep
Full of sweet dreams, and health, and quiet breathing.

Henry Wadsworth Longfellow

Henry Wadsworth Longfellow (1807–82) was an American educator, linguist, and poet. Incredibly bright as a child, he graduated from college at age nineteen. After studying in Europe for a time, he began his career as a college professor of modern languages. A legend in his own time, his poetry was widely appealing because of its universal themes and accessible language. He is the only American poet to have been honored with a bust in Westminster Abbey's poet's corner. His epic "Song of Hiawatha" represented the sympathy he felt for the plight of the Native Americans.

The Song of Hiawatha

Thou the wild-flower of the forest!
Thou the wild-bird of the prairie!
Thou with eyes so soft and fawn-like!
If thou only lookest at me,
I am happy, I am happy,

As the lilies of the prairie,
When they feel the dew upon them!
Sweet thy breath is as the fragrance
Of the wild-flowers in the morning,
As their fragrance is at evening,
In the Moon when leaves are falling.
Does not all the blood within me
Leap to meet thee, leap to meet thee,
As the springs to meet the sunshine,
In the Moon when nights are brightest?
Onaway! my heart sings to thee,
Sings with joy when thou art near me,
As the sighing, singing branches
In the pleasant Moon of Strawberries!

Percy Bysshe Shelley

Percy Bysshe Shelley (1792–1822) wins the complicated love life award. At the age of eighteen, this son of a minor English aristocrat married Harriet Westbrook, the sixteen-year-old daughter of a tavern owner. Several years later, he left her and took up with Mary Godwin (more commonly remembered as Mary Wollstonecraft Shelley, the author of *Frankenstein*). As Shelley no longer believed in exclusive love, they invited Harriet and Mary's half-sister, Claire Clairmont (Byron's lover), to join their household. After Harriet drowned herself, Shelley wed Mary. But that didn't stop him from taking up a public flirtation with the common-law wife of his friend Edward Williams. He and Williams both later drowned in a boating accident.

The Indian Girl's Song
I arise from dreams of thee
In the first sleep of night—
The winds are breathing low
And the stars are burning bright.
I arise from dreams of thee—
And my spirit in my feet
Has borne me—Who knows how?
To thy chamber window, sweet!—

William Wordsworth

William Wordsworth (1770–1850) lived a long and largely conventional life. His close friend and neighbor was Samuel Coleridge, and the two spent many days and nights working on their poetry, to the point where it is sometimes difficult to discern who wrote what.

My Heart Leaps Up
My heart leaps up when I behold
    A rainbow in the sky;
So it was when my life began;
So it is now I'm a man;
So it be when I shall grow old,
    Or let me die!
The Child is father of the Man;
And I could wish my days to be
Bound each to each by natural piety.

Chapter 10
Vows for Uncertain Times

Because fate has no consideration for wedding planning, you may be facing a crisis like an imminent military deployment or the illness or recent death of a loved one. Perhaps you and your fiancé come from differing religious traditions and are having difficulty finding a middle ground for your vows. Here are some tips you can use and examples you can incorporate to mark the solemnity of the occasion without forgetting the joy.

Patriotic Words

If you or your fiancé is in the military, you may want to honor that commitment by including a verse of patriotic poetry or prose in your ceremony. This is a happy occasion, so choose something that is optimistic and uplifting. Here are some favorites. The authors range from presidents to pencil-pushers, but they are all very moving.

My Land

My land is where the kind folks are,
And where the friends are true,
Where comrades brave will travel far
Some kindly deed to do.
My land is where the smiles are bright
And where the speech is sweet,
And where men cling to what is right
Regardless of defeat.
My land is where the starry flag
Gleams brightly in the sun;
The land of rugged mountain crag,
The land where rivers run,
Where cheeks are tanned and hearts are bold
And women fair to see,
And all is not a strife for gold—
That land is home to me.
My land is where the children play,

And where the roses bloom,
And where to break the peaceful day
No flaming cannons boom.
My land's the land of honest toil,
Of laughter, dance and song,
Where harvests crown the fertile soil
And thoughtful are the strong.
My land's the land of many creeds
And tolerance for all
It is the land of splendid deeds
Where men are seldom small.
And though the world should bid me roam,
Its distant scenes to see,
My land would keep my heart at home
And there I'd always be.

—**Edgar Guest**

Fact

Edgar Albert Guest (1881–1955) was born in Britain and emigrated to Michigan with his family ten years later. After his father died, Guest dropped out of school and took a full-time job at the *Detroit Free Press*. Guest was a prolific poet, and in 1952 he was named Michigan's poet laureate, the only individual ever to hold the honor.

A Nation's Strength

What makes a nation's pillars high
And its foundations strong?
What makes it mighty to defy
The foes that round it throng?
It is not gold. Its kingdoms grand
Go down in battle shock;
Its shafts are laid on sinking sand,
Not on abiding rock.
Is it the sword? Ask the red dust
Of empires passed away;
The blood has turned their stones to rust,
Their glory to decay.
And is it pride? Ah, that bright crown
Has seemed to nations sweet;
But God has struck its luster down
In ashes at his feet.
Not gold but only men can make
A people great and strong;
Men who for truth and honor's sake
Stand fast and suffer long.
Brave men who work while others sleep,
Who dare while others fly . . .
They build a nation's pillars deep
And lift them to the sky.

—**Ralph Waldo Emerson**

ⓔ *Essential*

Writer, educator, abolitionist, and former Unitarian minister Ralph Waldo Emerson (1803–82) was a man who took the "till death do us part" line of his wedding vows very seriously. He was so affected by the death of his beloved young first wife, Ellen, that he visited her grave daily and eventually named his eldest daughter by his second wife after her.

Hail, Columbia

Hail! Columbia, happy land!
Hail! ye heroes, heaven-born band,
Who fought and bled in freedom's cause,
And when the storm of war was gone,
Enjoyed the peace your valor won;
Let independence be your boast,
Ever mindful what it cost,
Ever grateful for the prize,
Let its altar reach the skies.
Firm, united let us be,
Rallying round our liberty,
As a band of brothers joined,
Peace and safety we shall find.
Immortal patriots, rise once more!

Defend your rights, defend your shore;
Let no rude foe with impious hand,
Invade the shrine where sacred lies
Of toil and blood the well-earned prize;
While offering peace, sincere and just,
In heaven we place a manly trust,
That truth and justice will prevail,
And every scheme of bondage fail.
Sound, sound the trump of fame!
Let Washington's great name
Ring through the world with load applause!
Let every clime to freedom dear
Listen with a joyful ear;
With equal skill, with steady power,
He governs in the fearful hour
Of horrid war, or guides with ease
The happier time of honest peace.
Behold the chief, who now commands,
Once more to serve his country stands,
The rock on which the storm will beat!
But armed in virtue, firm and true,
His hopes are fixed on heaven and you.
When hope was sinking in dismay,
When gloom obscured Columbia's day,
His steady mind, from changes free,
Resolved on death or liberty.

—**Joseph Hopkinson**

Ⓔ *Fact*

Joseph Hopkinson (1770–1842) was a son of Francis Hopkinson, one of the signers of the Declaration of Independence. The younger Hopkinson was an attorney who successfully defended Supreme Court Justice Samuel Chase in his impeachment trial and served two terms in the House of Representatives.

One Country

After all,
One country, brethren! We must rise or fall
With the Supreme Republic. We must be
The makers of her immortality;
Her freedom, fame,
Her glory or her shame—
Liegemen to God and fathers of the free!
After all—
Hark! from the heights the clear, strong, clarion call
And the command imperious: "Stand forth,
Sons of the South and brothers of the North!
Stand forth and be
As one soil and sea—
Your country's honor more than empire's worth!"
After all,
'Tis Freedom wears the loveliest coronal;

Her brow is to the morning; in the sod
She breathes the breath of patriots; every clod
Answers her call
And rises like a wall
Against the foes of liberty and God!

—**Frank L. Stanton**

Fact

Frank L. Stanton (1857–1927) was the poet laureate in Georgia from 1925 to 1927 and wrote popular poems for the *Atlanta Constitution* newspaper. He frequently used dialects and characters that idealized the antebellum south.

Not Alone for Mighty Empire
Not alone for mighty empire,
Stretching far o'er land and sea;
Not alone for bounteous harvests,
Lift we up our hearts to Thee.
Standing in the living present,
Memory and hope between,
Lord, we would with deep thanksgiving
Praise Thee most for things unseen.

Not for battleship and fortress,
Not for conquests of the sword
But for conquests of the spirit
Give we thanks to Thee, O Lord;
For the priceless gift of freedom,
For the home, the church, the school;
For the open door to manhood
In a land the people rule.
For the armies of the faithful,
Souls that passed and left no name;
For the glory that illumines
Patriot lives of deathless fame;
For our prophets and apostles,
Loyal to the living Word;
For all heroes of the Spirit
Give we thanks to Thee, O Lord.
God of justice, save the people
From the clash of race and creed,
From the strife of class and faction;
Make our nation free indeed.
Keep her faith in simple manhood
Strong as when her life began,
Till it finds its full fruition
In the brotherhood of man.

—**William P. Merrill**

> William Pierce Merrill (1867–1954) was a Presbyterian pastor who wrote poems and hymns. "Not Alone for Mighty Empire" is actually a hymn Merrill wrote in 1911 set to music by the eighteenth-century Austrian composer Franz Josef Haydn. It also works nicely by itself as a poem.

A Signer Declares

There is a tide in the affairs of men, a nick of time. We perceive it now before us. To hesitate is to consent to our own slavery.

That noble instrument upon your table, that insures immortality to its author, should be subscribed this very morning by every pen in this house. He that will not respond to its accents, and strain every nerve to carry into effect its provisions, is unworthy of the name of free man.

For my own part, of property, I have some; of reputation, more. That reputation is staked, that property is pledged on the issue of this contest; and although these grey hairs must soon descend into the sepulcher, I would infinitely rather that they descend

thither by the hand of the executioner than
desert at this crisis the sacred cause of my
country.

—**John Witherspoon**

Ⓔ *Fact*

Scotsman John Witherspoon (1723–94) was a
Presbyterian pastor who moved his family to New
Jersey to lead what became Princeton University.
Witherspoon served in the Continental Congress
and was an enthusiastic signer of the Declaration of
Independence. In retaliation, the British burned his
library, and he also lost a son in the battle of Ger-
mantown. Actress Reese Witherspoon is one of his
descendants.

A Congressman's Prayer
Almighty Father! look in mercy down:
Oh! grant me virtue, to perform my part—
The patriot's fervour, and the statesman's art
In thought, word, deed, preserve me from thy frown.
Direct me to the paths of bright renown
Guide my frail bark, by truth's unerring chart,
Inspire my soul, and purify my heart;
And with success my stedfast purpose crown.

My country's weal—be that my polar star—
Justice, thou Rock of Ages, is thy law—
And when thy summons calls me to thy bar,
Be this my plea, thy gracious smile to draw—
That all my ways to justice were inclin'd—
And all my aims—the blessing of mankind.

—**John Quincy Adams**

Ⓔ Essential

The sixth president of the United States, John Quincy Adams (1767–1848), had a long and illustrious career in the House of Representatives after serving one term in the White House. Known as "Old Man Eloquent," he spent the latter part of his career in Congress working for civil liberties.

The Americans' Creed

I believe in the United States of America as a government of the people, by the people, for the people; whose just powers are derived from the consent of the governed; a democracy in a republic; a sovereign nation of many sovereign states; a perfect union, one and inseparable; established upon those principles of freedom, equality, and humanity for which American patriots sacrificed their lives and fortunes.

I, therefore, believe it is my duty to my country to love it, to support its constitution, to obey its laws, to respect its flag, and to defend it against all enemies.

—**William Tyler Page**

𝕰 *Fact*

An enthusiastic patriot and lifelong public servant, William Tyler Page (1868–1942) was a descendant both of president John Tyler and Carter Braxton, a signer of the Declaration of Independence. His "Americans' Creed" was compiled of phrases pulled from numerous historic documents, and the House of Representatives adopted it in 1918. It is part of the naturalization ceremony for U.S. citizens.

Letter to Martha

It has been determined in Congress, that the whole army raised for the defence of the American cause shall be put under my care, and that it is necessary for me to proceed immediately to Boston to take upon me the command of it.

You may believe me, my dear Patsy, when I assure you in the most solemn manner that, so far from seeking this appointment, I have used every endeavor in my power to avoid it, not only from my unwillingness to part with you and the family, but from a consciousness of its being a trust too great for my capacity, and that I should enjoy more real happiness in one month with you at home than I have the most distant prospect of finding abroad. . . .

It was utterly out of my power to refuse this appointment, without exposing my character to such censure as would have reflected dishonor upon myself, and have given pain to my friends. . . .

I shall rely, therefore, confidently on that Providence which has heretofore preserved and been bountiful to me, not doubting but that I shall return safe to you in the fall.

—George Washington

Fact

Martha Dandridge Custis (1731–1802) met George Washington when she was in the enviable position of being one of the wealthiest and most beautiful young women in Virginia. As a widow, she had sole control of her fortune, a perk she would have to give up if she remarried. But marry George she did—after only five meetings—and by all accounts, theirs was a loving, faithful union of forty-three years.

Lift Every Voice and Sing
Lift every voice and sing
Till earth and heaven ring,
Ring with the harmonies of liberty.
Let our rejoicing rise

High as the list'ning skies;
Let it resound loud as the rolling sea.
Sing a song full of the faith that the dark past has taught us;
Sing a song full of the hope that the present has brought us;
Facing the rising sun
Of our new day begun,
Let us march on, till victory is won.
Stony the road we trod,
Bitter the chast'ning rod,
Felt in the days when hope unborn had died;
Yet, with a steady beat,
Have not our weary feet
Come to the place for which our parents sighed?
We have come over a way that with tears has been
watered;
We have come, treading our path through the blood of the
slaughtered,
Out from the gloomy past,
Till now we stand at last
Where the white gleam of our bright star is cast.
God of our weary years,
God of our silent tears,
Thou who hast brought us thus far on the way;
Thou who hast by thy might
Led us into the light:
Keep us forever in the path, we pray.
Lest our feet stray from the places, our God, where we met
thee;

Lest, our hearts drunk with the wine of the world,
  we forget thee;
Shadowed beneath thy hand
May we forever stand,
True to our God, true to our native land.

—**James W. Johnson**

An abridged list of the accomplishments of renaissance man James Weldon Johnson (1871–1938) includes educator, writer, anthropologist, lawyer, activist, musician, and diplomat. He originally wrote the words to "Lift Every Voice and Sing" for a celebration recognizing Abraham Lincoln's birthday. In 1919 the NAACP adopted the song as "The Negro National Anthem." Part of the beauty of the piece is that it can be interpreted to mean any number of things.

The "Worse" Part of "For Better or for Worse"

Life throws curve balls at the most inconvenient times. Maybe your favorite uncle just died, or your fiancé's sister was recently diagnosed with a serious disease. The good news is, most etiquette books no longer mandate the cancellation or postponement of a wedding if something like this happens. On the other hand, if you feel that postponing is the right thing to do, don't hesitate to let people know. They will understand. As your friends and family, many of them will be grieving right along with you.

Ⓔ Alert!

In 2001, when former James Bond actor Pierce Brosnan's teenaged son was seriously injured in a car accident days before his dad's scheduled wedding, the bride and groom put off the ceremony for two months until the youngster was well on the road to recovery.

As you already know, planning a wedding can be stressful all by itself. If you throw in a medical crisis on top of that, you can quickly feel like you're circling the drain. If you have already decided to take part in premarital counseling, use your counselor to help you deal with the added strain. If you need a special grief therapist, ask for a referral. If you don't have a counselor, call a local house of worship, hospital, or hospice. They'll point you in the right direction, pronto.

Times of crisis can pull couples apart or draw them closer. You want to be one of the latter. Find the silver lining in your situation and use the opportunity to build up the trust and strength of your relationship by going the extra mile for each other. Take time to decompress; go for walks or see a movie, anything to help you forget for a while and recharge your batteries.

If you or someone you love is facing a major life event, you and your guests may feel better just by acknowledging the 800-pound gorilla in the room. Hopefully you'll never find yourself in such a situation, but if you do there are a lot of poems that address tragedy or love that transcends death. Including such a piece in your wedding may be a much-needed relief valve that lets people feel free to express their sadness amidst their joy. Here are a few examples that might strike the right chord.

All Return Again

It is the secret of the world that all things subsist and do not die, but only retire a little from sight and afterwards return again.

Nothing is dead; men feign themselves dead, and endure mock funerals and mournful obituaries, and there they stand looking out of the window, sound and well, in some new strange disguise. Jesus is not dead; he is very well alive; nor John, nor Paul, nor Mahomet, nor Aristotle; at times we believe we have seen them all, and could easily tell the names under which they go.

—**Ralph Waldo Emerson**

Ⓔ *Fact*

Ralph Waldo Emerson's first wife, Ellen, was only twenty when she died of consumption after less than two years of marriage. Emerson's passionate first marriage eventually gave way to a relationship based more on respect with his second wife, Lydia. Perhaps he named his eldest daughter with Lydia, Ellen, in the hope that she might be the reincarnation of his first wife.

Tecumseh's Teaching

Live your life that the fear of death
can never enter your heart.
Trouble no one about his religion.
Respect others in their views
and demand that they respect yours.
Love your life, perfect your life,
beautify all things in your life.
Seek to make your life long
and of service to your people.
Prepare a noble death song for the day
when you go over the great divide.
Always give a word or sign of salute when meeting
or passing a friend, or even a stranger, if in a lonely place.
Show respect to all people, but grovel to none.

When you rise in the morning, give thanks for the light,
for your life, for your strength.
Give thanks for your food and for the joy of living.
If you see no reason to give thanks,
the fault lies in yourself.
Touch not the poisonous firewater that makes wise ones
turn to fools and robs the spirit of its vision.
When your time comes to die, be not like those
whose hearts are filled with fear of death,
so that when their time comes they weep and pray
for a little more time to live their lives over again
in a different way.
Sing your death song, and die like a hero going home.

—**Tecumseh**

Fact

Tecumseh (1768?–1813) was a member of the
Shawnee tribe in central Ohio. A charismatic leader
and fearless warrior, he worked hard to prevent the
collapse of the Native American resistance against
white settlers. He was eventually killed in a battle
against the Americans (led by future president William Henry Harrison).

If Death Is Kind

Perhaps if death is kind, and there can be returning,
We will come back to earth some fragrant night,
And take these lanes to find the sea, and bending
Breathe the same honeysuckle, low and white.
We will come down at night to these resounding beaches
And the long gentle thunder of the sea,
Here for a single hour in the wide starlight
We shall be happy, for the dead are free.

—**Sara Teasdale**

Fact

American poet Sara Teasdale (1884–1933) was well known in the early part of the twentieth century for her writings about death, love, and nature. Never able to live with the passion she expressed in her writings (and possibly depressed by the recent suicide of a former lover), Teasdale took her own life after a debilitating bout of pneumonia.

Peace, My Heart

Peace, my heart, let the time for the parting be sweet.
Let it not be a death but completeness.
Let love melt into memory and pain into songs.

*Let the flight through the sky end in the folding of the wings
    over the nest.*
*Let the last touch of your hands be gentle like the flower of
    the night.*
*Stand still, O Beautiful End, for a moment, and say your
    last words in silence.*
*I bow to you and hold up my lamp to light you on your
    way.*

—**Rabindranath Tagore**

Ⓔ *Fact*

Born into a wealthy Brahmin family in Calcutta, Rabindranath Tagore (1861–1941) managed his family's estates and wrote poetry. In an effort to ward off boredom on a long sea voyage to England in 1912, he translated some of his poems into English. The famed poet W.B. Yeats helped him get published, and the next year Tagore won the Nobel Prize for literature.

Chapter 11
Gay and Lesbian Wedding Vows

It's only been recently that the possibility of legally sanctioned same-sex marriage has been on anyone's radar in the United States. In this brave new world, many couples may feel like they're making it up as they go. Some choose to give specific voice to the challenges their love has endured. Others want to put the past behind them. But all vows focus on the love that the couple shares for each other and their commitment to forging a life together.

Wedding Versus Commitment Ceremony

There are still precious few places where a gay or lesbian couple can legally get married. As of press time they were limited to California and Massachusetts. In these places, homosexual married couples' rights and responsibilities are no different from those of their heterosexual brethren.

Many other states offer civil unions or same-sex partner benefits. In some cases, these are the same as marriage, just disguised under a different name. In others, they are limited to one or two privileges, such as being allowed to share your partner's health insurance. Because this is a very fluid issue, check with an attorney in your state to make sure you thoroughly understand what the law says and what these programs mean for you and your partner and children.

You can also conjoin spirits in a feel-good but not legally binding commitment ceremony. Many houses of worship are happy to sponsor these partnerships, offering the same kind of premarital counseling and guidance that they do to straight couples. It won't have the legal import of a legislatively sanctioned wedding or civil union, but a good attorney can wade through the reams of paperwork necessary to make sure you and your beloved are trussed together as tightly as your state's laws allow.

Ⓔ *Essential*

Print out the words you want spoken for the service. Some clergy think quickly on their feet, but you don't want to cringe every time you watch your wedding video and hear, "Do you, Albert, take Roger to be your lawfully wedded wi—I mean, husband?"

Regardless of the legal technicalities of your union, the vows you speak should take on the same eternal sacredness as those of any other wedding.

Quotes about Love

Many wedding vows are gender neutral and can be used for any couple, but you can make your wedding vows stand out from the average heterosexual couple's. You can incorporate quotes from notable LGBT authors like Walt Whitman, Audre Lorde, or Sappho. It's only been very recently that writers have been labeled according to their sexual orientation. Many people feel that love is love and doesn't have to be defined by gender or sexual orientation. After all, very few of the quotations from the previous chapters speak of specifically heterosexual love. In the end, it doesn't matter as much who originally wrote the words; who is saying them to whom and the emotions behind them are what matter the most.

The love expressed between women is particular and powerful, because we have had to love in order to live; love has been our survival.

—Audre Lorde

A line can be straight, or a street, but the human heart, oh, no, it is curved like a road through mountains.

—Tennessee Williams

*Without warning
as a whirlwind
swoops on an oak
Love shakes my heart*

—Sappho

*Camerado, I give you my hand!
I give you my love, more precious than money,
I give you myself, before preaching or law;
Will you give me yourself? Will you come travel with me?
Shall we stick by each other as long as we live?*

—Walt Whitman

Where there is great love, there are always wishes.

—Willa Cather

When you're in love you never really know whether your elation comes from the qualities of the one you love, or if it attributes them to her; whether the light which surrounds her like a halo comes from you, from her, or from the meeting of your sparks.

—Natalie Clifford Barney

Once my heart was captured, reason was shown the door, deliberately and with a sort of frantic joy. I accepted everything, I believed everything, without struggle, without suffering, without regret, without false shame.

—**George Sand**

Keep love in your heart. A life without it is like a sunless garden when the flowers are dead. The consciousness of loving and being loved brings a warmth and richness to life that nothing else can bring.

—**Oscar Wilde**

Ⓔ *Fact*

Oscar Wilde was an Anglo-Irish nineteenth-century writer and wit who was tried and imprisoned for his homosexual relationship with the son of an aristocrat. It was widely believed that he was unfairly made an example of, as his behavior was not uncommon in that time.

Is love a light for me? A steady light,
A lamp within whose pallid pool I dream
Over old love-books? Or is it a gleam,
A lantern coming towards me from afar
Down a dark mountain? Is my love a star?
Ah me!—so high above so coldly bright!
The fire dances. Is my love a fire
Leaping down the twilight muddy and bold?

Nay, I'd be frightened of him. I'm too cold
for quick and eager loving. There's a gold
Sheen on these flower petals as they fold
More truly mine, more like to my desire.
The flower petals fold. They are by the sun
Forgotten. In a shadowy wood they grow
Where the dark trees keep up a to-and-fro
Shadowy waving. Who will watch them shine
When I have dreamed my dream? Ah, darling mine,
Find them, gather them for me one by one.

—**Katherine Mansfield**

To live is like to love—all reason is against it, and all
healthy instinct for it.

—**Samuel Butler**

All human beings are also dream beings. Dreaming ties all
mankind together.

—**Jack Kerouac**

Writing Unique Vows

Most wedding vows can be used for both heterosexual
and same-sex ceremonies with minor alterations. You can
change the pronouns and a few key phrases ("husband
and wife" easily becomes "partners in life") and call it a
day, but many couples want more than that.

In writing your own vows, you may want to draw particular attention to your same-sex union. One way of doing
this is to allude to the adversity you have faced and your
partner's role in helping you through it. Your wedding offi-

ciant may have some suggestions based on what other couples before you have done. Here is one example:

❦ You are my best friend and constant companion. Your heartfelt compassion and unwavering love have guided me through uncertain times. Today we join our lives. I will always be by your side, ready to share in every success and every obstacle. I promise to faithfully love, trust, and respect you from this day forward.

Whether you choose to incorporate quotes or write your own wedding vows from scratch, you have a great deal of freedom to express yourself and your feelings.

Chapter 12
Vows for Renewals or Subsequent Marriages

You learned a lot during your first marriage: good, bad, and ugly. The negative lessons were undoubtedly as instructive as the positive ones, but they have no place in your new wedding vows or renewals. It's best to leave out specifics like "I will take out the garbage without being asked," and concentrate on more general positives such as "You taught me how to laugh, hope, and enjoy life again." If either of you have minor children, including them in vow renewal or subsequent wedding is a good way to get the entire family involved.

Renewing Your Vows

People renew vows for a lot of reasons, but most fall into two categories: to reiterate a successful long-term commitment or to give a fresh start to a fractured relationship.

Weaving the Tapestry of Your Lives

If you're planning on renewing your vows for the sheer joy of it, you already know you have much to be grateful for: someone you can count on to clean the cat vomit that you pretend not to notice and someone who can read your mind with eerie accuracy (and who doesn't hold it against you).

Ⓔ *Essential*

There is no mandated time for renewing vows. Most couples wait for a landmark anniversary, although some eager couples renew their vows on their first anniversary. You can do it after as few as ten years, or as many as seventy-five.

In addition to publicly stating your love and support for your spouse, look upon this ceremony as an opportunity to inspire others. Remember the time your husband was laid up from work and you had to work two jobs to keep the boat afloat until he was well again? Or how about the time you were convinced your wife was having an affair because she couldn't account for all of her spending money, and it turned out she was socking it away so she could surprise you with a cruise? These are the kinds of experiences that only come with miles on the odometer, but sharing them with your children and grandchildren can give them a leg up wisdom-wise in their own relationships.

No one knows better than you two what you've been through over the course of your marriage. Even if you don't want to write all of your vows, jot down some memories and thoughts to personalize the event. The officiant at your ceremony (which can be anybody from your priest to your pedicurist, because this is not a legal conjoining of lives) can open the ceremony by relating one or two of these enlightening and/or amusing anecdotes from your time together. Your vows should reiterate your successful marriage and emphasize what you have learned and been grateful for and that you would do it all over again.

Healing a Hurt Marriage

We're all human, and sometimes we act badly and hurt the ones we love the most. If you have successfully mended a terrible rift in your marriage, you may want to take the opportunity to renew your vows and acknowledge the new strength of your relationship. Your counseling and hours of reflection have probably given you a good start for your vows. You've learned a lot about yourself, your spouse, and your relationship, and you can incorporate it all into your affirmation.

Making a Fresh Start

When it comes to crafting vows for these occasions, it helps to sit down and make a list of why you want to renew your vows. Ask yourself questions like:

- How is our love different now from when we first married?
- How have my spouse and I changed over the years and made each other better people?
- What are his or her best qualities?
- What do I promise to do going forward?

Leave out negative references. "George, I forgive you for sleeping with my cousin" is not quite the note you want to strike. Try instead, "George, we are both human and both capable of erring and worthy of earning forgiveness."

This is the place for optimistic statements like "I have learned" and "I will always try" and words like *affirmation, blessing, caring, compassion, experience, growth, harmony, joy, pledge, promise, proud, together, trust*. The past is behind you. This ceremony is about the present and the future.

Subsequent Marriages

If this is your second (or more) stab at marriage, you probably already have plenty of experience under your belt. That puts you far ahead of the curve.

Celebrating the Wisdom that Comes with Experience

Lucky you. Against the odds, and maybe even your own expectations, you've met someone so special that you're ready to take the plunge again.

Thanks to your accrued experience you have some idea of what to expect. You know that people have good days and bad days and that neither will really factor into the big equation. Make sure your spouse-to-be knows this too. Take turns being each other's rock.

Positive phrases to incorporate in your subsequent wedding vows might include: "eyes wide open," "let go of the past," "look forward to the future," "love/laugh/embrace life again," "one true love," "second chance at happiness," "secure in the knowledge," "start anew," "without reservation." Just like with the vows for any other wedding, it's an invaluable exercise to jot down what is unique and what you love about this person and your relationship.

What Not to Include

A good marriage counselor will encourage you to put the lessons you've learned from earlier relationships to positive use in your new one. But don't harp on the past. This is the time to concentrate on the positive. Remember and repeat as necessary, "the past is behind me, this is all about the present and the future."

When an Entire Family Makes a Vow

Some children accept stepparents with open arms; others need a little (or a lot) of coaxing. One way to help them make this adjustment is to continue to spend lots of alone time with them and encourage them to talk honestly and openly about their feelings and concerns. In your turn, you should be open and honest with them.

Ⓔ *Question?*

What if my kids hate my intended?
It's okay for children to express a little resentment toward a prospective stepparent, but if your children are up in arms, listen to them carefully. Ask specific questions. It's your job to listen to and address their concerns. If they really can't engage with their new family, it's time to call in a professional counselor to help smooth the transition.

One way to reiterate the cohesiveness of your new family unit is to include everyone in a family vow. This can be something like a mass lighting of a unity candle or a family sand ceremony. For the former, you can have all the members of the family (if they're old enough) light the candle at the same time. If that's too nerve-wracking, you can have the children light their parent's candle and then have the adults light the unity candle together. In a sand ceremony, all members of the family, regardless of age, can pour a handful of sand into one container. The commingled grains represent the new family.

Some families are also incorporating a family medallion into their vows. Once the parents and children have made their promises to each other, the parents present each child with a piece of jewelry with three interlocking rings, representing the parent, stepparent, and child(ren) who are now united as a single family.

 Alert!

If you're presenting your child with a memento of the event, consider making it an inexpensive and easily replaceable token. Children like to play with their new toys, and no one wants to be unduly upset if the item should break or go missing. Save the sterling for when they're adults.

Vows to Include Children

Uniting two partners who have children from previous relationships is about more than a marriage. It creates a family. To acknowledge the exceptional nature of the marriage, some couples like to include their children in the ceremony. This gets children involved in the wedding, and they play a central role because they essentially bless the union of their parent and stepparent.

Vows for Younger Children

You or your officiant can create vows that are age-appropriate and that might reflect your own vow. It's

probably best not to ask the kids to memorize anything. Younger children can either repeat a vow after
an officiant or say "I do" after the officiant reads the
vow.

- Officiant: Marjorie and Henry, do you promise to love,
  honor, and respect your father's new wife and support
  them in their marriage?
- Marjorie and Henry: We do.

Vows to Children

It's equally important for the new stepparent to publicly declare his intention to love and support the new
child or children. It doesn't have to be elaborate, just one
or two sentences to assure the kids that you love and cherish them as your own and will be a support to them forever. The stepparent might consider kneeling down to the
kids' eye level and telling them how much both the new
spouse and the children mean to him, how proud he is to
be joining the family, and that he will love and help the
children for the rest of their lives. If that doesn't bring tears
to everyone's eyes, nothing will.

The couple can read a passage about family and
togetherness from a classic book or the stepparent can
read a vow promising to love the child or children.

- Lola, today I promise to love, cherish, and honor your
  mother as my wife. I love you, too, and I pledge to

take care of you as my own child. We will be a happy family together, and we will share many fun times.

Ⓔ *Essential*

Very few new families settle into their new roles seamlessly. An advice columnist once suggested that new stepparents treat love more like an action and less like an emotion because your actions are a lot easier to control. When the emotion finally does follow, it will be the real thing.

Vows for the Whole Family

To make the ceremony more personal, stepparents can write a few words about each child. Older children can respond to their stepparent's vows with personalized vows of their own. You can help children write the vows or you can let them express themselves.

- ❦ Josie, I love your fun-loving spirit, and I promise to keep you safe as we explore new worlds together. Edmund, I love your independent character, and I promise to respect your boundaries as we grow as a family together.
- ❦ Tim, you understand our family and I am excited to call you my stepfather. I promise to love you and respect your relationship with my mom.

The vows do not have to directly respond to one another. Older children have a greater understanding of their parent's feelings, and they may want to thank their stepparent for making their parent happy.

Quotes about Family

It's a nice touch to have children read a favorite passage from a book or a quote that relates to family. You may have your own favorites, but here are some suggestions.

In time of test, family is best.

—**Burmese proverb**

Ohana means family, and family means nobody gets left behind or forgotten.

—***Lilo and Stitch***

The love of a family is life's greatest blessing.

—**Unknown**

In every conceivable manner, the family is link to our past, bridge to our future.

—**Alex Haley**

There's no vocabulary
For love within a family, love that's lived in
But not looked at, love within the light of which
All else is seen, the love within which
All other love finds speech.
This love is silent.

—**T. S. Eliot**

Call it a clan, call it a network, call it a tribe, call it a family. Whatever you call it, whoever you are, you need one.

—Jane Howard

Love. That was what she had that IT did not have.

—Madeleine L'Engle

Appendix A
Traditions from Around the World

Vows are one way of personalizing your ceremony, but there are thousands of wedding traditions from around that world that are just waiting to be incorporated into your wedding. You don't have to belong to the culture from which it originated, but it is a unique way of paying homage to your heritage if you choose.

African

There are more than 1,000 different cultures represented on the African continent. Central to all African weddings is the joining of two families. Divorce is very rare among traditional African couples. The husband's and wife's families and even whole tribes will come together to help the couple work out their differences and ensure that the union thrives.

A few customs are easily incorporated, like the twelve symbols of African life that are often represented in wedding ceremonies. They include bitter herbs, a broom, honey, pepper, a pot, salt, a shield, a spear, a spoon, water, wheat, and wine. Perhaps the best known is the jumping of the broom. This Ashanti custom started in Ghana; waving brooms over the heads of the married couple warded off evil spirits. When Africans were enslaved and brought to the Americas they were forbidden from marrying. A secret jump over the broom witnessed by friends and relatives often sufficed to wed couples who had fallen in love.

In Kenya, the night after the wedding, the women get together to celebrate with the bride in a *kupamba*, a ceremony in which the bride "enters" the world of married women. They eat, drink, and make merry with music and laughter.

European

Many familiar traditions came from Europe like white wedding dresses (which actually represent prosperity, not virginity) and the kiss (a Norwegian exchange of souls).

Celtic Traditions

The Celts literally tied the couple's hands together in a ceremony called handfasting. Thus came the tradition of "tying the knot." They also threw pebbles into a body of water in order to create ripples, which were considered good wishes radiating out to the couple.

England

The saying "something old, something new, something borrowed, something blue" originated in England. The symbols represented continuity in the circle of life, hope for the future, luck from an already happily married couple, and purity. Ancient Israeli brides also wore something blue in their bridal costume; it represented fertility.

France

In many small French towns, the groom goes to the bride's house and escorts her to the church. Small children will sometimes stretch white ribbons in front of them that the bride must cut. Every bride has a sprig of orange blossom in her bouquet to symbolize virginity. French couples stand underneath a silk canopy called a *carré* in order to protect them from bad luck and drink from a two-handed cup called a *coupe de marriage* that is handed down in families through the generations.

Some couples will forgo a wedding cake for a more traditional *croquembouche*, which is a pyramid made of crème-filled pastries with a glaze over the top. French revelers also enjoy banging pots and pans under the window of newlyweds. Once the couple plies them with alcohol, the noisemakers usually depart.

Greece

Greek wedding guests smash their plates in the belief that the more pieces they break into, the happier the couple will be. Greek couples wear their gold bands on their left hands during their engagement, then switch to the right after they're married.

Ireland

Irish couples walk through their town on their way to the church. Revelers throw rice at them—and sometimes heavier items like pots and pans! Traditional Irish brides often wear blue, the ancient symbol of purity, and include English lavender in their bouquets to represent luck and loyalty.

Getting married on St. Patrick's Day was traditionally considered the ultimate good luck charm for Irish brides and grooms. Sprinkle some four-leaf clovers in your wedding bouquet and boutonnieres, and add something in your vows about how you will be as brave for each other as St. Patrick was when he ran away from his slave master and returned home to his family.

Italy

In order to protect them from evil spirits, an Italian groom might carry a piece of iron in his pocket, and the bride will cover her face with a veil. While couples walk to church, onlookers will put obstacles in the bride's path to see how she reacts to difficulties in life. Italian brides traditionally had bread or cake broken over their heads to ensure fertility.

Poland

In Poland, the groom and his parents show up at the bride's home to pick her up and take her to the church. At this time, both sets of parents give the couple their blessings.

When the couple gets to the church they process up the aisle together, followed by two witnesses and their parents. It is very rare to see a gaggle of bridesmaids and ushers. The parents greet the couple at the reception with bread to symbolize abundance, salt to symbolize the adversities they will have to overcome, and wine to symbolize the happiness they will experience together.

Scotland

Scottish couples usually depart their wedding ceremony to the sound of bagpipes. Male guests will frequently wear a bit of white heather in their buttonhole to symbolize good luck.

After the ceremony, the groom pins a piece of his clan's tartan on his new wife's dress to symbolize that she is now part of his family. Scottish grooms lift their brides over the threshold of their new home to protect them from the evil spirits that reside there.

Asia

Asia proper is a huge place, and the cultures it encompasses are many and varied.

China

Red is a very important wedding color. It represents prosperity, happiness, and love. The bride's traditional wedding dress, present wrappings, and other elements are often red. Before the wedding, the bride and groom serve tea to both sets of parents. After the wedding, brides serve tea to their new in-laws.

Chinese couples traditionally get married on the half-hour instead of the top of the hour so that they start their life together on an upswing. Wedding cakes are made of many layers, representing the ladder to success that the couple will climb together. A young boy bounces up and down on the bridal bed to ensure that the couple has a male heir.

India

Eggs, sweets, and money are common themes in Indian weddings, representing, fertility, a happy life together, and financial success. Indian brides wear red or sometimes pink saris on their wedding days. Before the wedding, brides are "cleansed" and have elaborate designs painted on their hands and feet in henna. Hindu grooms wear turbans hung with flowers over their faces to protect them from evil spirits.

Japan

A Japanese bride is painted white from head to toe to display her purity. She also wears a white kimono and a headpiece that is draped with good luck charms. Grooms wear black kimonos.

During the traditional Shinto ceremony the two families stand facing each other. During the ceremony, the bride and groom take part in the *san-san-kudo* ritual. Three cups are stacked on top of one another; the top cup represents heaven, the middle cup represents Earth, and the bottom cup represents humans. The bride and groom pour sake into the first cup, and each takes three sips. The process is repeated for the other two cups. The family also drinks to unite the two clans.

Korea

Korean brides are pelted by their fathers-in-law with red dates, which represents fertility. Ducks and geese are common wedding symbols. Both species mate for life and represent fidelity.

Russia

Russian brides and grooms "race" each other to the special carpet they stand on when they recite their vows. Legend has it that whoever reaches it first will be the head of the household.

Upon drinking a toast to the new couple, the guests throw their champagne glasses on the floor. The more glasses that break, the better luck the newlyweds will enjoy.

The Americas

Because Canada and the United States are countries that were predominately settled by immigrants, there are many variations on the "traditional" wedding. Fortunately, there are many rich indigenous cultures that can offer alternatives to the traditional Anglo-Saxon wedding theme.

Argentina

Argentinean couples exchange rings at their engagement, not at their wedding. They also eschew attendants, preferring that the father of the bride and mother of the groom support them during the ceremony.

Mexico

Couples planning to marry are sponsored during their engagement and marriage by their godparents. During the wedding the couple is lassoed by a white ribbon or rosary to symbolize their unification.

A groom traditionally gives his wife thirteen gold coins, which the priest has blessed, as a symbol of his commitment to support her during their marriage. Guests shower the newlyweds with red beads to wish them luck.

Native American tribes

Among the Akwesasne people, when a younger sibling married first, the elder siblings had to do a special dance in a pig trough.

An Algonquin bride bathed in a body of water on the morning of her wedding in order to be blessed by the spirit of the earth. The couple gave a wedding gift to each of their guests. There was no divorce among the Algonquin. Even if a couple separated, they were still considered married.

Cherokee couples exchanged a deer ham and an ear of corn to indicate the husband's willingness to provide for his bride and the woman's willingness to be a good wife. During the ceremony they were each covered with separate blue blankets and then finally one white blanket to symbolize their new united life together.

Young couples in the Delaware area often just took up housekeeping together with the blessings of their parents. For the traditional exchange of gifts a young bride would paint her face with white, red, and yellow clay.

If a young Hopi woman wanted to propose, she would offer the object of her affections a loaf of *qomi*, bread made of sweet cornmeal. If a young man wished to propose he would prepare a bundle of fine clothes and deerskin moccasins and leave it at her door.

Among the Navajo people white corn represented males and yellow corn represented females. Cornmeal of both colors was mixed together into a mush and, in keeping with their tradition of equality between the sexes, the couple would eat it as part of their wedding ceremony.

Puerto Rico

Like the Mexican coin tradition, the Puerto Rican groom has the priest bless a plate of coins, which he then gives to his new wife. It is not an uncommon sight for a doll covered in charms and dressed as a bride to be placed on the head table. These charms are later passed out to the guests as gifts.

Appendix B
Resources

Books

Cotner, June. *Wedding Blessings: Prayers and Poems Celebrating Love, Marriage and Anniversaries.* (New York, NY: Broadway Books, 2003).

Evans, Ann Keeler. *Promises to Keep: Crafting Your Wedding Ceremony* (Rites to Remember Series). (Philadelphia, PA: Emerald Earth Pub., 2001).

Foley, Michael P. *Wedding Rites: The Complete Guide to Traditional Vows, Music, Ceremonies, Blessings, and Interfaith Services.* (Grand Rapids, MI: Eerdmans Publishing Company, 2008).

Johnson, Judith. *The Wedding Ceremony Planner: The Essential Guide to the Most Important Part of Your Wedding Day.* (Naperville, IL: Sourcebooks, Inc., 2005).

Kaplan-Mayer, Gabrielle. *The Creative Jewish Wedding Book: A Hands-On Guide to New & Old Traditions, Ceremonies & Celebrations*. (Woodstock, VT: Jewish Lights Publishing, 2004).

Lavender, Shonnie and Mulkey, Bruce. *I Do! I Do! The Marriage Vow Workbook*. (Asheville, North Carolina: self-published, printed by Lulu, 2006).

Naylor, Sharon. *Renewing Your Wedding Vows: A Complete Planning Guide to Saying "I Still Do."* (New York, NY: Broadway Books, 2006).

Roney, Carley. *The Knot Guide to Wedding Vows and Traditions: Readings, Rituals, Music, Dances, and Toasts*. (New York, NY: Broadway Books, 2000).

Warner, Diane. *Diane Warner's Complete Book of Wedding Vows: Hundreds of Ways to Say "I Do."* (Franklin Lakes, NJ: The Career Press, 2006).

Wright, H. Norman. *The Complete Book of Christian Wedding Vows: The Importance of How You Say I Do*. (Ada, MI: Bethany House Publishers, 2001).

Websites

Brilliant Wedding Pages

A fantastic online resource about writing your own wedding vows; includes a helpful worksheet.
www.brilliantweddingpages.com/couples /weddingvows.asp

Perfect Wedding Vows in Minutes

This website features Mad Lib-style wedding vows.
www.perfect-wedding-vows.com/weddingvow.htm

ForeverWed.com

This website has links to dozens of wedding vows.
www.foreverwed.com/religious_ceremonies/

Mahalo.com

This website has a good step-by-step process for writing your own wedding vows.
www.mahalo.com/how_to_write_your_own _wedding_vows

The Knot

This all-inclusive wedding website includes an entire section on the ceremony and vows.
www.theknot.com

I Do Take Two.com

This entire website is devoted to subsequent marriages. There is a section on the ceremony and vows.
www.idotaketwo.com

Love to Know

"Funny" wedding vows to laugh at, but not to use!
weddings.lovetoknow.com/wiki/funny_wedding_vows

LGBT-Friendly Church Organizations

Dignity

This organization supports the LGBT community within the Catholic church.
http://dignityusa.org

The Gay Christian Network

This nonprofit ministry is devoted to the Christian LGBT community.
www.gaychristian.net

Integrity

This organization is committed to the LGBT community in the Episcopalian church.
http://integrityusa.org

Metropolitan Community Churches

This international church welcomes LGBT members.
http://mccchurch.org

Seventh Day Adventist Kinship

This Adventist group advocates for LGBT members within the church.
http://sdakinship.org

Index